THE DEPTH OF HER SURVIVAL

HEALING FROM NARCISSISTIC
ABUSE AND COERCIVE CONTROL

TRACEY GRACE

First published by Ultimate World Publishing 2023
Copyright © 2023 Tracey Grace

ISBN

Paperback: 978-1-922982-28-5
Ebook: 978-1-922982-29-2

Tracey Grace has asserted her rights under the Copyright, Designs and Patents Act 1988 to be identified as the author of this work. The information in this book is based on the author's experiences and opinions. The publisher specifically disclaims responsibility for any adverse consequences which may result from use of the information contained herein. Permission to use information has been sought by the author. Any breaches will be rectified in further editions of the book.

All rights reserved. No part of this publication may be reproduced, stored in or introduced into a retrieval system, or transmitted in any form, or by any means (electronic, mechanical, photocopying, recording or otherwise) without the prior written permission of the author. Any person who does any unauthorised act in relation to this publication may be liable to criminal prosecution and civil claims for damages. Enquiries should be made through the publisher.

Cover design: Ultimate World Publishing
Layout and typesetting: Ultimate World Publishing
Editor: Vanessa McKay
Cover Image Copyright: lassedesignen-Shutterstock.com

Ultimate World Publishing
Diamond Creek,
Victoria Australia 3089
www.writeabook.com.au

Contents

Preface v
Introduction 1
Chapter 1: My Landing Place 7
Chapter 2: Filling the Void 17
Chapter 3: Early Warning Bells 25
Chapter 4: If You Are Not Okay, I Am Not Okay 39
Chapter 5: Entrapment 43
Chapter 6: Generational Trauma 55
Chapter 7: The Downward Spiral 77
Chapter 8: The Point of No Return 91
Chapter 9: Look What You Made Me Do 97
Chapter 10: The Courage to Jump 123
Chapter 11: If I Can't Have You I Will Destroy You 131
Chapter 12: The Monster Under the Mask 149
Chapter 13: The Discard 157
Chapter 14: A Harrowing Survival 163
Chapter 15: Invisible Chains and Flying Monkeys 183
Chapter 16: Will I Ever be Free 199
Chapter 17: Riding the Waves 211
Chapter 18: Phoenix Rising 215
Chapter 19: Pain into Power, Wounds into Wisdom 227
Chapter 20: The Way Forward 233
Author Bio 239
References 241
Trauma Release Session 245
Phoenix Rising – Trauma Healing Program 247

Preface

Through this book, I am sharing my personal journey of hitting rock bottom after finding myself trapped in a toxic and controlling marriage. The frightening escalation of abuse that occurred through the post-separation period when I finally left the relationship led to a brutal and soul destroying three and a half year battle, fighting for freedom and safety through various court systems. This experience woke me up to the frightening level of corruption, injustice and incompetence that commonly occurs through the very systems that are ultimately supposed to protect partners or children who are at risk of suffering domestic violence[1], yet often result in the escalation of risk and insurmountable damage to the lives of those attempting to leave an abusive relationship.

My experience of this relationship and the post separation abuse that followed resulted in the loss of everything I had ever known, at the hands of a vindictive and controlling ex-partner. An experience that I thought I would not survive. An experience that stripped away any hope that I would ever find freedom, stability, or happiness again. An experience that I genuinely feared would take my life.

I have leaned into the immense vulnerability it has taken to voice my story through this book and to share my intimate experience of survival and healing from the debilitating trauma of narcissistic abuse and coercive control, covert and insidious forms of domestic violence. As a single mother with two young children, isolated and in the absence of a support system, I have navigated, and crawled my way through the depth of relentless pre and post-separation abuse that stripped my world of every ounce of stability, safety, support, freedom and hope that I had.

Through this toxic and controlling relationship, I experienced so much loss in all aspects of my life. I lost the foundations of my health, my family, my lifelong friends, my career, my financial security, my sense of self, my confidence, and at times what felt like my mind.

Our beautiful children lost so much in their early childhood years. They lost the chance to develop mentally and emotionally in a calm and stable environment. They lost their sense of belonging within a family unit, their right to have stability and a secure place to call home, their belief in what healthy relationships look like, and their idea of what unconditional love from both parents is and should be. There were times our children saw and heard things no young child should be exposed to. They lost a part of their innocence. They missed out on a sense of belonging and connection within an extended family unit. They lost their right to live in a calm and peaceful environment. It robbed them of their birth-right, to feel safe in this world and receive unwavering, unconditional love for the precious and worthy humans they are.

I have since rebuilt our life from scratch. I have walked barefoot right through the very flames that were set to destroy me, and I have risen from the ashes. I have established security, safety and freedom once again to the extent I can within the circumstances, not only externally in my outer world but also within myself and the core of who I am. I have developed a newfound wisdom and strength that will forever be a part of me and can never be taken away. I have such profound clarity of who I am now, what I stand for, and a deep knowing of my worth that is continuing to evolve.

Preface

I am proud of who I have become as a woman and mother and the cycles of generational dysfunction that I am conscious of breaking for the future of our children and for those who come after me.

Through my adversity, I have found my life's purpose: to help others find their voice, to tap into their inner strength, to activate their intuition, to realise their worth and to reclaim their power. And to use this transformation to navigate the aftermath of leaving an abusive relationship, surviving the debilitating post-separation abuse that typically follows and to step into the powerful, sovereign and worthy human they have always been.

Since stepping out of this toxic and abusive relationship, I have become a Trauma-Informed Mental Health Practitioner after embarking on extensive study of multiple science based and complementary modalities. I now use not only my knowledge and skills from years of training but also my life experience and finely tuned intuition, to support people who are in the throes of leaving and trying to heal from not only the impact of their abusive relationship but also their lifelong trauma, childhood conditioning, limiting beliefs and unhealthy patterns that predisposed them to those experiences and relationships in adulthood.

My desire for this book is to connect with as many of you as possible who have been traumatised from narcissistic abuse, coercive control or any other form of domestic violence, whether through an intimate partner or other relations, and to ensure that at the end of reading this book; you know you are not alone in what you have endured and that the abuse that happened to you is real. I hope you can release with grace and ease those people, whether family, friends or professionals who side with your abuser or invalidate your experience, and that no matter what injustice may occur through the legal and court systems, that you trust the innate strength that lies within you to carry you through to the other side of the destruction. My wish is that you will know with every ounce of your being that you are worthy of having a voice and being BELIEVED for what has happened to you. That you will access the strength within you to reclaim your power and transform your trauma into wisdom. That you will remember who you are, and never allow someone to make you feel less than ever again.

I vow to be a support, mentor and advocate and lead with courage and conviction, for those who follow me in this brave step of leaving an abusive relationship, and to be a soft place to fall for those who haven't quite found the courage to take this frightening step just yet.

To all my valued readers who relate to my story…

I see you, I hear you, I believe you…and you are not alone.

You can and will have joy, freedom, and peace once again. That is my promise to you.

I will be with you each step of the way.

Tracey Grace ♡

Preface

"You either walk inside your story and own it, or you stand outside your story and hustle for your worthiness." Brene Brown

Introduction

Narcissistic abuse and coercive control are insidious forms of domestic violence. Going through it is a lonely, confusing, and terrifying experience. There are so many forms of abuse at play: emotional, psychological, financial, sexual, or physical. You often spend many years dealing with an individual who has maliciously and intentionally created a relational prison, where they perpetrate patterns of coercive and controlling behaviour to maintain power within the relationship dynamic[2]. This typically involves gaslighting, contradicting, put-downs, accusations, criticism, blaming, bullying, pathological lies, infidelities, manipulation, dehumanisation, projections, demanding, raging, shaming or threatening[2]. Amongst this are breadcrumbs of short-lived highs, love bombing, ingenuine promises, and good times that give you just enough hope to keep you holding on and believing that things will change for the better. There is so much deception and abuse that is hidden that you lose your ability to trust yourself. It's like living in a constant fog.

You experience a complete erosion of your self-esteem and self-confidence, chronic nervous system dysregulation, and the depletion of your vital life force energy. Even as I write this, I know the only people who will really understand what I'm talking about are those that have gone through it themselves. This is not just a bad relationship experience or two people who are incompatible or have grown apart. This is the murder of a person's spirit. It's the dismantling and destruction of a life, intentionally, one piece at a time. And as you are trying to hold it together, people who don't understand domestic abuse or the resulting trauma are looking on and judging you, like you are going crazy or there is something wrong with you. And at times it feels like you are going crazy and like there is something wrong with you, as you don't even understand what is happening anymore because the confusion, cognitive dissonance and depletion of your sense of self is so severe.

The relationship slowly breaks you apart and erodes everything you once were. It's a confusing and isolating experience to go through and my heart goes out to those still struggling to survive such dynamics and those trying to heal from the aftermath.

You will notice throughout this book that I use the terms "survivor" and "abuser" frequently to describe the roles within such toxic relationships. Although people who experience narcissistic abuse, coercive control or other forms of domestic violence are "victims" and did not choose or deserve such treatment, the term "survivor" allows those who have experienced such ordeals to place themselves in an empowered position in relation to their trauma and it best represents their strength in what they have endured. I believe that using the term "survivor" is a healthier representation for the individuals of such an experience rather than speaking to them as a "victim". The word "abuser" is a term that is used throughout this book to describe the intentional and harmful patterns of behaviour that a perpetrator of domestic and narcissistic abuse displays.

Introduction

There may be some that are reading this book who are not going through such an experience, but who want to educate themselves and better understand what a family member, friend, or client is experiencing in order to best support them. For those who are trying to support someone stuck in or having recently left a toxic or controlling relationship, it's so important to understand this message:

They did not allow, choose, or deserve the abuse. People who end up in these relationship dynamics are lied to and coerced into the abusive situations, and before they know it, their living situations, their financial security, their self-worth and all of their systems of support are infiltrated by their abuser. People don't choose to be abused. They are manipulated into believing they are going to be valued and cared for and by the time they realise it was all a lie and that they need to get out, they are so worn down and vulnerable, that it's too late to do so without tearing their entire world apart. It makes it very hard to leave.

So, if you are trying to support someone in an abusive relationship or through the post-separation period, be patient and have compassion. Understand that it is incredibly hard to take that step to leave for good. And when they take that step, expect that it will be tough and there will be trauma and heartache. There will be big reactions that seem irrational and periods of time they are stuck in what seems to be "victim mentality". You will probably hear strategically planted information from their abuser that may make you somewhat question and doubt their story. The escape and journey to get away from the relationship dynamic will be all-consuming, leaving them no space or capacity to focus on anything else for a while. Despite all this, support is critical. Support is also the number one thing that the abuser will target, and support is the number one thing that is needed to help a survivor make it through.

With the current climate of the legal and court systems, there will probably be victim blaming, further traumatisation and heartache from the very systems that are supposed to be there to protect and support. These systems are, unfortunately, a part of the problem. Your patience, your compassion and your non-judgemental and unwavering support are crucial. Someone who is in or has been in an abusive relationship doesn't need you to fix anything or provide unsolicited advice. They need to feel supported and to know they are not alone. They need you to BELIEVE them. I know without a doubt that this alone can make an enormous difference to the safety, wellbeing and lives of those trying to leave, survive and eventually heal from an abusive relationship.

Introduction

The most powerful words you can say to a trauma survivor are, I see you, I hear you, I believe you, and you are not alone.

CHAPTER 1

My Landing Place

Reflecting on the horrors of the abusive relationship dynamic I was stuck in for almost a decade, the highs and lows and the utterly terrifying post separation period, I finally have a deep sense of knowing that I have found my landing place, and that everything is going to be okay. I now have the wisdom and tools to ensure our children will be okay. As I share my story with you, our parenting arrangements have not yet been legally finalised because my ex-partner continues to stall. In fact, I have recently received notice of his intent to commence further family court proceedings following an extended period of complete radio silence after he reneged for a fourth time on an agreed mediation outcome for our parenting arrangements to be finalised. Despite these ongoing attempts to maintain control and intimidate me anyway possible, I have reached a point in my journey where I have healed to the level where I can give myself closure and take back control of my own life.

I have regained my personal power within the dynamic and have accepted it for what is, without being crippled by fear, and living in a disempowered state waiting for the hit of his next move. For the first time in as long as I can remember, I feel somewhat safe in my body and safe in this world. My nervous system is feeling glimpses of what it is like to experience small moments of calm and ease, and not live in a chronic state of fight and flight survival mode, day in, day out.

Residual anxiety still creeps in whenever he contacts me, when I have to deal with legal processes, when hearing that old friends continue to buy into his lies and fabricated narrative, or when the overwhelming realisation sets in of the enormous responsibility that lays ahead of me being a solo mother without a supportive or reliable co-parent. Reflecting on the fact I have single-handedly raised, cared for and provided for our children through this entire ordeal, gives me some comfort in that I have shown myself I have the ability to do it for the future if needed.

I still have insecurities and experience fear that he will suddenly manipulate or sway my remaining friends with his disingenuous charm to turn against me like so many others along the way.

There are also still some chronic health issues and physical symptoms I am working on healing as I unwind from the years spent in survival mode. I can say with certainty, however, that the strength and determination that resides within me now is unwavering.

To compensate for the fallout of our relationship and despite the chronic exhaustion of single parenthood and the relentlessness of needing to wear all and every hat to ensure our children have what they need, it has been a challenging yet willing choice to devote myself completely to our children.

With the fear of the unknown still lingering, and the very real chance he will continue to drag me through vexatious legal proceedings for years to come, I am in awe of how far I have come in my healing and my determination to transform my pain into power. Sometimes I honestly didn't feel like I was going to survive. The relentless abuse, the impact on my physical and mental health, the crippling isolation from all forms of support, and the genuine fear he wanted to, and early in our separation, was planning to "get rid of me" for good.

I recall the feeling of my body and nervous system literally shutting down from the immense chronic stress that was being created day in day out by my children's father. I didn't know how my mind was going to stay in-tact when every part of me unconsciously wanted to dissociate and shut down from the horrors at play. How my psyche didn't completely fracture or split through this time is beyond me, but it has shown me the resilience of the human spirit and the depth of tenacity a mother can have to stay strong for her children.

My children without doubt saved my life. When every part of me wanted to fall apart, both physically and mentally, I had no choice but to put one foot in front of the other and keep going. As I sit here today, I am proud of my courage and sheer determination to not let my children down. My fight for their safety and their future never wavered. Despite crippling fear and insurmountable heartache at the hands of their father, who showed time and time again he was out to destroy me at all costs, I never gave up on what was truly important - the safety, stability and wellbeing of our children.

Most people do not know what it is like to be stripped bare of everything you once knew, from basic security, safety, support, reputation, health, career and everything in between, and then crawl your way through the rubble of the destruction, with young and dependent children in tow. Although I'm through the darkest parts of the experience, I still feel such a sense of shock at the depth of what unfolded and that another human being, let alone the father of my children, could be capable of what I can only describe as pure evil. It continues to shock me to my core and will forever change me and my perception of this world with this unforgettable insight into the capacity and depth of darkness of those disordered individuals who roam undetected amongst our human race.

What is a narcissist?

I first want to acknowledge that placing a label or diagnosis on someone, such as "narcissist" can be controversial and sit uncomfortably for some. From my perspective and through a trauma-centred lens focused on supporting survivors, the purpose of using a label and giving it a name is not to define, shame or diagnose individual perpetrators, but to name the abuse to help survivors heal. Being able to name and define the abuse allows survivors to categorise what they have experienced, identify it as abuse and separate themselves and their worth from the toxic treatment.

The term "narcissist" sums up an evidenced and researched pattern of harmful behaviour that an abuser directs towards their "victim". Naming it allows survivors to detach from the belief that there is something wrong with them and that they deserved the harmful treatment. When survivors realise there is a well-established body of knowledge on this type of systemic abuse, they also realise that the abuse was not their fault and that there was nothing they could have done to change the outcome of the relationship. The world can make sense once again when they have the comprehension and language to describe what they have been through. It doesn't really matter how we label narcissists when they are not the beneficiaries of that label in the literature of narcissistic abuse. Using these terms can be powerful in helping survivors realise they are not alone and assist them in finding the information they need in order to separate their worth from the way they were treated, to overcome the abusive situation and therefore being able to heal.

We hear the term "narcissist" thrown around a lot this day and age, and almost every young girl who has a cheating or arrogant ex-partner will use the term narcissist to describe their experience. It has become the buzzword for someone who hurt or betrayed us. In reality, there is only a small percent of people in society who are true narcissists with Narcissistic Personality Disorder (NPD)[1] or other similar disorders associated with psychopathy or sociopathy such as Antisocial Personality Disorder[2]. When you come across such types, and their mask finally comes off, you will not be mistaken. It will make you wish all you had was a cheating ex-partner or a past partner that was arrogant and self-centred.

A true narcissist can be difficult to detect by those not in intimate relationships with them, and often difficult to detect by even those who are, until they are entrapped through marriage, children, or the onset of trauma bonding. They are brilliant and intelligent in the execution of their behaviour and show only their false mask, selecting their next victim and managing their image impeccably to the outside world. They live their life through their mask. Image management is everything. Not even their own family or friends often know who they really are underneath, although there are usually links with similar disorders somewhere in their upbringing, and those who stand by them and enable their behaviour are toxic and dysfunctional in themselves.

It's important to note that there are various types of narcissism and that it is a spectrum. There are those who operate in covert ways and those who are grandiose and more overt. There are narcissists who are also very malignant and can often have the deeper pathology of a psychopath or sociopath. Because of the calculated and strategic nature of a narcissist, their ability to lie pathologically and their professional manipulation skills, their behaviour is near impossible for most on the outside world to detect. Their actions are typically sinister, callous, covert, and strategically executed.

A common theme in narcissistic relationships is that they purposely cause confusion by creating two polar realities or experiences. A narcissist will strategically execute love bombing, charm, compliments and acts of love, followed by devaluing and purposely making their target feel inadequate and not good enough. This results in cognitive dissonance, which is extreme mental discomfort and confusion caused by two polar experiences, thus making it difficult for victims to distinguish which experience is indicative of the reality of the relationship.

Extremely calculating by nature, narcissists often strategise with precision in how to win the admiration, trust or respect of those they believe they can benefit from. They need to be admired by others and anything positive or generous they do is aimed at gaining recognition and is being done in the public light. They will only treat people well who they believe they can gain something from, who they perceive as above them or equal in status or who they see will make them look good from association with them. If someone attempts to hold them accountable for their behaviour and they are unsuccessful in manipulating them to see otherwise, they will embark on a vindictive smear campaign conducted ever so subtly and with the right level of fake remorse to make their false narrative believable by their targeted audience.

They are extremely self-serving and everything is about gaining their own desires and needs at the expense of those they exploit to get there. They are very jealous of other people's success. They need narcissistic supply and cannot be alone. They feed off the energy, reactions, and admiration of others. They can maintain a façade and mask to those outside the intimate relationship ongoing and continue to show only the qualities that they know will be accepted and win admiration. It is for this reason it can be extremely hard for others to understand or comprehend the depth or truth of what a survivor has experienced within the relationship.

The sad part is that narcissism typically stems from childhood trauma and conditioning and has a direct correlation to a person's upbringing. There are also theories that the development of narcissism may stem from genetics and DNA, or from spiritual and psychic aspects where a person becomes detached from their soul and have been taken over by a lower consciousness or entity that drives their behaviours. The link with childhood trauma and conditioning is undeniable however, and the challenging part for "victims" of such people is not to fall into the trap of feeling sorry for them or excusing their behaviour. Your compassion for understanding their childhood experience can cause you to become stuck in the cycles of abuse by people who will only take advantage of an empathetic and forgiving partner and continue to exploit them.

What is coercive control?

People often think of domestic violence as physical harm. Although it is common for physical harm to be present in this type of dynamic, with any physical domestic violence, coercive control[3] is always present. Coercive control can be present with no physical harm occurring. This is the most difficult type of domestic violence to detect from the outside. Those who experience coercive control in a relationship often don't even realise that they are a victim of domestic violence. One of the most challenging things about coercive control and helping those experiencing this insidious form of abuse, is that the legal and court systems, police and other professionals who are supposed to protect vulnerable people in society who are victims of domestic violence, are often not equipped, to recognise or address coercive control and leave the victim even more at risk, traumatised and vulnerable than before they were involved.

All too often, a part of an abuser's tactic is to flip the narrative, re-write history and create a scenario where the true victim is isolated, seen as "unstable" and is perceived as the problem. This is often accompanied by false allegations made against them and intentional triggering of the trauma they developed from the occurrences in the relationship to make them look unstable and abusive in their reaction. It is typical for them to create a false narrative behind the scenes to their friends and family to justify why they did the things they did so if the abuse is ever mentioned after a survivor leaves the relationship, the narcissist has already gotten in first with the false narrative and therefore it makes it difficult for people to believe the true victim when they finally speak out. It is like being burnt at the stake for something you didn't do or being portrayed as a character you are not. The more disempowered and crippled you become through these experiences, the more powerful, in control and invincible the narcissist feels.

Abusers who use coercive control know exactly what they are doing and the more reactive and upset you get from their conduct towards you, the more it feeds their desire for power over you. The more they see the evidence that they can fool even the most experienced professionals within the system, the more their behaviour will escalate. They feel invincible. They genuinely believe they are above the law. This feeds their need to feel powerful and in control and typically escalates their behaviour to levels that a person with a conscience would not even get close to being capable of.

In relationships, it is often hard to detect for many years that what you are experiencing is coercive control, as abusers are masters of manipulation and keep you stuck in cycles of abuse mixed with love bombing and good times that have you stuck in a state of confusion and holding onto hope for change. These cycles cause you to become biochemically addicted to the combination of stress hormones of adrenaline and cortisol and bonding hormone, oxytocin. There is always chronic gaslighting keeping you in a frozen internal state of despair and confusion about what is happening to you and holding you in a negative belief about yourself, slowly eroding your self-esteem. Your growing weakness is their strength. They need you powerless so they can be in control and feel powerful. This is their ultimate goal in entering a relationship. They target those who are compassionate, kind hearted and often those who are carrying unhealed trauma and wounds that result in them sacrificing their own needs or people pleasing in order to maintain connection and love at all costs. If you end up in a coercive, controlling relationship, you were strategically hand-picked for the role and it is no mistake that they know exactly what they are doing to your sense of self, confidence, and self-worth.

CHAPTER 2

FILLING THE VOID

I met my ex-partner in my early thirties at a time I had spent well over a decade dedicated to a high tempo and intense career that had been my primary focus. As much as I loved my career and felt satisfied with my life achievements, I felt burnt out and imbalanced in life with the strong pull and almost unhealthy need to find a life partner and to catch up with everyone else my age in establishing a family. I recall feeling such discomfort as I attempted to slow down in life and my career, in the way I was feeling inside myself. Although very capable and highly independent, I wasn't content on my own. I didn't feel whole. It felt as if something was missing, and I desperately needed to fill the void and distract myself from my inner world. It was as if the moment that I slowed down from the go-getter life, the underlying and undeniable discontentment seeped through.

On reflection, I can see how I had been distracting myself my whole life. With career, adventure, partying, and achievements. I also realised that ever since my father passed away in my early twenties, I had been on the go without stopping. Five days after he died, and after battling to get time off work from the army to get home for his funeral, they shipped me off interstate to live for three months for a residential promotion course. No-one knew me, no-one knew I'd just lost my father. I pretended I was fine. I kept busy. I suppressed my emotions. I worked hard, and I partied hard. I realise now that I did not have the tools, support or guidance to express or process my difficult emotions. I'd never been modelled this. There was no one there to support me through the grief process and it was all brushed under the rug and life moved on. I recall even on the day of my father's funeral, as my sisters and I carried his coffin down the aisle at the cemetery to the burial site, my primary focus was to make sure I didn't show emotion. It was like being vulnerable, expressing emotion or voicing my needs did not and had never been safe or accepted. I had adopted a belief that I had to be strong and keep people at arm's length at all times. I had an armour and façade, and no one could see inside. I therefore suppressed any emotions and shut off to and disconnected from my inner self. Little did I know this would be the start of a long and undetected downward spiral in my life, with chronically unprocessed and suppressed grief at the core, combined with dysfunctional beliefs about my self-worth and value as a person. I just didn't stop until about ten years later to actually feel it, and when I slowed down, I couldn't deal with the suppressed emotions residing within me so I tried to fill the void and the way I did this was to go on a mission to find my life partner to feel whole. I realise now that this feeling of discontentment and longing for something external to make my internal state feel better was a key aspect that led me to settling and blatantly ignoring the red flags that were present from early in our dating period.

I have learnt that the unhealed parts of myself from my childhood, that always felt unloved, unworthy, not good enough, not supported, not valued and not accepted for who I was, was always searching for something outside of myself to validate my worth. These associated parts of myself led to co-dependent behaviours and ultimately trauma bonding and were the underpinning of my entrapment within this dysfunctional relationship. It was the perpetuation of the cycles of abuse within the relationship that strategically targeted and further eroded my self-worth and confidence, resulting in trauma bonding and making it feel impossible to get out of.

Trauma bonding results when you're so heavily attached to a toxic person that you will maintain a relationship, even at the expense of your health, happiness and safety, while holding onto the few highs and good times. Your brain becomes highly addicted to the habitual ups and downs of oxytocin, dopamine, norepinephrine, and serotonin that even on attempts to leave the relationship because you cognitively know it's unhealthy, you will seek and crave the person back, or seek similar people in order to get your fix. It's a dysfunctional rewiring of the neurological pathways of love and turning against itself.

Losing "love" and attachment makes you crave them more. You are biochemically dependent in the same way someone addicted to a substance is. This is one reason it is typically so hard to leave an abusive relationship and research[1] shows it takes someone, on average, seven attempts to leave a toxic relationship for good.

In trauma bonding in adult relationships, there is nearly always a link to childhood and an insecure attachment to a primary caregiver and a core subconscious belief that you are not good enough and that you need to sacrifice your needs to gain love and acceptance. This same desire and need for an attachment is playing out when you remain in an abusive relationship. In addition, there is the repeating of the familiar patterns of abuse and love co-existing, or emotional unavailability and love co-existing. This contributes to trauma bonding and carries through within your neurology and nervous system to adulthood until you ultimately find yourself in a familiar pattern with an adult partner. We unconsciously gravitate to adult partners who provide us with a familiar feeling to what we experienced in our attachments or environments as a child. This remains the case until we heal and resolve the associated beliefs and let go of the unhealthy conditioning established in childhood.

We can become almost addicted to a partner who is unavailable or abusive and who doesn't choose us. This is because we have a wounded inner child who is still trying to get our primal needs met for attention, connection, and love that were not met as a child. It is ultimately our subconscious trying to seek safety. The toxic partner we fixate on is someone who, to our subconscious mind and inner child, reminds us of the environment we experienced as a child where we did not get the love, attention, and emotional availability we needed. We learned to associate love with unavailability and longing, rather than availability and having.

Sometimes, we may have learnt to associate love with abuse. So, when someone is unavailable or abusive, it feels familiar to what we know as love. This is because the way this person is showing up mirrors the pattern of emotional unavailability or abusive treatment that we experienced with caregivers or witnessed in our childhood environment. This doesn't always mean you were abused, it can also be the things that were not done and the absence of the things you did not receive, unconsciously and unintentionally by caregivers who didn't know any better, didn't have capacity to do better and were playing out their own unhealed trauma.

We as humans have "repetition compulsion" [2] which is a process that keeps us repeating the same patterns that match our unhealed wounds with the aim to finally get what we didn't get in childhood to heal these wounds. Our inner child and subconscious are still seeking to have our unmet needs met through the dysfunctional yet familiar patterns. For those who are more spiritual, we can also understand it to be our soul searching for the experiences needed to heal our wounded parts and, therefore, be able to evolve as a spiritual being.

In childhood, if you did certain things and performed in certain and accepted ways, then you may have received acknowledgement, praise, or sometimes avoided abuse or abandonment. This instilled a core belief that you must work and perform for love, as it wasn't experienced as something unconditional or freely given. Because of this, you feel at the core of who you are, that you are not good enough. This instilled an understanding that you need to change who you are and make yourself good enough in order to deserve love; ultimately gaining the safety in connections you innately need. With these unhealed parts from childhood, meeting someone in adulthood who is unavailable and who doesn't choose us or harms us, triggers this *I need to work harder and be who they need me to be* pattern hoping if we do, we will finally be good enough and receive that love and connection that every human innately needs to feel safe. Obsessing over making them happy, chasing, sacrificing our needs, stepping into controlling or dysfunctional ways to gain a sense of safety and security from a connection with them, and overworking for this unavailable or abusive person, is a direct manifestation of this belief system.

Fixating and obsessing on changing who we are and pleasing and appeasing this unavailable or abusive person is the way our inner child is subconsciously trying to get our needs met. It is an attempt to feel safe through a fantasy bond. These feelings of longing, desperation and fear of abandonment that are triggered by this person, is our inner child trying to fill our need for love and connection by holding onto a fantasy of who this person is or could be. It is just that. A fantasy and imaginary connection that does not bring safety and love, but quite the opposite.

Just the same way, that as a child, you may have grown up feeling alone, unsupported, unloved, and not seen and heard. In your inner child's fantasy, this abusive or unavailable person who feels energetically familiar, gives glimpses of hope through love bombing, breadcrumbs of inconsistent loving behaviour, future faking and false promises, and therefore gives a distorted hope for finding the safety and connection you have desperately wanted all your life. Your perception is that they hold the key to you finally being seen, heard, loved, and valued. This fantasy, in conjunction with cognitive dissonance, has you believing that this person is the one who can meet the needs of the inner child that was not met in childhood. The subconscious believes that this person who mirrors the caregiver or household environment in which you grew up in will finally bring the wholeness and healing your inner child is subconsciously seeking.

This is not reality and is a dysfunctional thought pattern that will keep you stuck in unhealthy dynamics. It is near impossible for this dynamic to bring the safety and connection that you are seeking, as it is based on dysfunctional beliefs. The intense "love" or more accurately feeling of infatuation or neediness, is precisely because you are feeling their emotional unavailability and it is the associated insecure or unhealthy attachment style you have, that is driving the intense need to maintain a connection with this person. This is merely an attempt to gain security in your attachment and can be mistaken for feelings of intense love. When unconditional and consistent love was not received in childhood, there is no point of reference to determine what healthy and genuine love actually is or feels like. This feeling of intense longing and inability to let go of an unavailable or abusive person can become an addiction that you can become trapped in for years; unless you do the healing work to break the cycle.

If you can relate to this pattern in relationships and find yourself infatuated, fixated, or unable to let go of someone who hasn't chosen you and who is unavailable or abusive, it is a sign that you are experiencing trauma bonding. You may have an insecure attachment style and negative subconscious beliefs about yourself and a wounded inner child who is desperately seeking to be seen, heard, validated, and loved. It's an indication that unhealed childhood trauma is playing out in your adult life. It's coming to the surface in patterns, symptoms and experiences so it can be healed. So you can return to the wholeness within yourself by turning inwards to tend deeply to the unhealed parts of you that have been unconsciously playing out as patterns in your life, and in particular, your resulting abusive relationship.

I can see now how I was strategically selected by my ex-partner, like a predator eyeing off its prey, not only for my financial assets, but for the unhealed parts of me that craved connection, acceptance, approval, stability and unconditional love. It was like he sensed my vulnerabilities and could see how my loyal and empathetic nature, along with people pleasing tendencies and poor personal boundaries, would make me a prime source of "supply" for him. I was the perfect target for a narcissist to feed their obsession for control, and for their self-serving behaviour to be excused and forgiven repeatedly through carefully calculated cycles of love bombing, devaluation, discard and hoovering. In hindsight, the depth of lies and manipulation that I experienced from the very beginning was extreme and at levels that I can only describe as professional, calculated, and that of a master.

CHAPTER 3

Early Warning Bells

At the time of meeting my ex-partner on a dating site, he lived in a different state. I was seeking a life partner, and I told him directly that I was only interested in investing my time in something serious and that the long distance and casual arrangement he indicated wasn't for me. He was very persistent and began insisting he was also looking for a long-term relationship. I always felt a sense of mistrust or like something wasn't quite right, but disregarded this in my intense desire for finding my companion in life and instead listened to his words rather than looking at his actions and behaviours. My gut feeling and intuition were trying to warn me, but the excitement and love bombing that occurred in these initial times overshadowed the underlying unease that I felt.

The ecstasy and excitement he created to lure me in was irresistible and he wouldn't take no for an answer. I perceived this as a complement to his interest in me as a person and that I was someone extra special to him.

It wasn't long before things changed and progressed to phases of feeling like I was insignificant and of the least importance to him. It was such a stark contrast and shifted so quickly that it was incredibly confusing. I felt insecure and consumed with trying to regain what I thought we had and ensure I was enough for him. I thought *I needed to try harder to keep him interested in me*, as if there was something wrong with me that I needed to change. This feeling that I needed to change who I am and try harder to gain approval in order to maintain connection, and avoid rejection or abandonment, would become one of my biggest revelations in unravelling the undeniable link between my childhood conditioning and my unhealthy relational patterns in adulthood.

As a teenager and adult, I was drawn to avoidant and emotionally unavailable men or those that were highly controlling and self-centred. I have since learnt that I had an insecure attachment to my primary caregiver in childhood that resulted in an unhealthy attachment style that continued into my adult relationships.

As children, when we feel our primal need for a secure attachment and bond to a caregiver is threatened, we change and adopt our behaviour to do what we think we need to in order to get connection and validation from others. We disconnect from our authentic self as we develop a belief that who we are is not accepted or lovable. We become highly attuned to reading the cues and appeasing or pleasing others to be accepted and avoid rejection. This is a trauma and survival response and stems from an innate and primal need to feel connected and safe. It is unconsciously carried into adulthood and becomes a hard-wired way of being. It becomes our perceived personality. This is where the "good girl" mentality and people pleasing traits come into play.

The need to people please is a trauma response that is developed in childhood. It is a coping mechanism and adaptation of personality, but is not the true essence of who we really are. It is a mechanism in how to cope and seek a sense of safety. It presents as having to do everything right, be perfect all the time and having hyperawareness of other's needs and wants. We become adults living out our childhood trauma by adopting a survival mechanism of appeasing others to avoid rejection and abandonment. Although this coping mechanism helped us survive as a child, it can create immense suffering in adulthood. It keeps us disconnected from our authentic self and keeps the pattern of low self-worth cycling through our life experiences.

Being excluded or amongst conflict can feel terrifying to the nervous system of a person with a childhood trauma of rejection, abuse or abandonment. It can feel as though it is a direct threat to survival through the loss of a bond and connection with others. According to research, our body and nervous system respond to perceived threat and trauma with common survival behaviours or stress responses: fight, flight, freeze or fawn[1]. It's common to seek safety by avoiding conflict, pleasing others and engaging behaviours to appease and pacify others by "fawning" when feeling under threat. Some may react from anger and aggressively appearing to create conflict when the "fight" response is triggered. Many will also adopt the "freeze" response and shut down, dissociate, and withdraw, feeling unable to move and oblivious to reality. Others may become avoidant, run away, push others away or call things off in the heat of the moment and have the urge to run away or escape by adopting the "flight" response as their survival adaptation. We can move between all four different survival responses and it's helpful to understand what these survival responses are and have an awareness of what they feel like, so we can recognise these trauma driven coping mechanisms and behaviours when they are playing out during times of stress.

I recall a time early during our dating phase when asking about his previous relationship that he had recently come out of. His response was that his ex-girlfriend, who was a doctor and a surgeon, was mentally unstable and crazy and that's why the relationship didn't work out. I sensed a subtle alarm bell on hearing this, but being so disconnected from my intuition and the lack of trust I had in myself, I disregarded it. I've since reflected on not trusting my inner knowing and not paying attention to the signs my body gives me when I know something to be untrue or a danger to be present. I can clearly see how I was impacted by my childhood experiences.

I was exposed to gaslighting and criticism from a young age. If I ever had the courage to speak up to dysfunction and if I dared to voice an opinion or belief, that was different to my family of origin, they saw it as a threat. If I saw, heard or felt something I knew to be true, I was often told I was making it up, that I was overreacting, and was constantly told I was too sensitive. There were times I was framed to be a liar to the rest of my family by a caregiver to cover up for what I knew. My personal power and intuition were a threat. They were squashed and suppressed until they existed no more.

I grew up learning not to trust my inner knowing and intuition and I could not recognise and act on red flags in my adulthood. This has been one of my greatest lessons through my recovery and healing from narcissistic abuse; learning to trust my intuition and follow my gut feeling. It's ALWAYS there. It has always been there. I just needed to learn to recognise it, take notice, and listen to it.

Another red flag that my ex-partner demonstrated early in our relationship that continued and escalated well into our separation, was that he would go behind my back and have conversations about our issues with my support network. All without my knowing, without sharing the actual truth and with intentions of manipulating them to see him as a caring partner and subtly paint me as troubled or the issue.

After dating for a few months, he phoned my mother, who he'd only met on two occasions, after we had issues around him drinking excessively and repeatedly having all night benders at strip clubs. He phoned her without my knowledge, telling her he was concerned about me while failing to share the truth of why we were arguing. He continued to groom her and sweet talk her into believing he genuinely cared for me and was a good guy who was concerned about me. He requested that she not disclose to me he had contacted her. This allowed for his false narrative and grooming to go undetected by me and painted him as a caring and concerned partner to those of my support network. This same pattern of behaviour used to occur frequently with my then best friend as well.

He contacted my close friends to discuss our relationship issues without sharing the truth of why we were having issues, all while portraying concern for me and requesting they don't tell me they had spoken. It created a scenario over the years in which they developed trust in him for the façade he showed them, as he planted subtle seeds of doubt in them about me. This grooming of my support network began very early on and the path to set up compete isolation from any support if I ever left him was well planned and executed with precision during our separation.

Despite the early warning bells and red flags in our dating phase, I continued to enjoy the fun when we caught up and naturally tried to deepen our connection as time went on. I recall one evening when we had been coasting along for quite some time, that I asked him a simple yet profound question to get to know him on a deeper level. I asked him what his three top core values were. His response was like a bucket of cold water to the face and couldn't be ignored for the giant red flag it was. Once again, I chose to avoid and disregard this and hold on to my fantasy that he might be the one. His response to my question on what his top three core values were: *work, blow outs and fun*. He clarified "blow outs" as being big nights out partying. It was like hearing that someone had no depth, direction or substance to them, yet he continued to insist he wanted a relationship, commitment and to settle down with me. At this stage, I still believed this man could connect emotionally to another person with time, but little did I know it would become one of the biggest and longest battles in our relationship. I was seeking and striving for emotional connection with someone who did not have the emotional capacity, availability, or genuine empathy to connect with another human being.

It wasn't long before I discovered the infidelity that had been ongoing and the lack of monogamous commitment to me, he had previously claimed. Because we were living in separate states and I now could see that the relationship wasn't going anywhere, I called it off as it was negatively impacting me more than adding value. It had all become very consuming and was affecting my health and my productivity at work. I was definitely hurt and felt upset that I had wasted my time and that it wasn't what I was hoping for or he had promised it to be.

Following my attempt to call it for what it was and finish the relationship, he immediately switched his behaviour with intensity and focused on sucking me back into the toxic relationship cycle, with an almost prophetic declaration of his love and how he only saw his future with me. His attention increased to almost unnatural levels; artificially filling my desire to be loved and valued.

Once hooked back in, through a manipulation tactic known as "hoovering", the same cycle would occur again. Hoovering is a behavioural tactic used by a toxic person who is attempting to manipulate you to resume contact with them or to step back into the relationship when they are trying to fill a void or need, or they fear you are getting away[2]. This can look like intense declarations of love for you, lavish gifts, future promises, fake remorse, and basically not taking no for an answer with a relentless insistence that they won't let you go because of their genuine love for you. Another couple of months passed before I saw the same evidence and the same behaviour reoccurring.

I soon discovered another infidelity. This time because he had basically forced me to stay with him after the last occurrence, and to then have a repeat of the very behaviour that he had witnessed hurt me so deeply, I ended things abruptly. The betrayal trauma of words not matching actions and being told blatant lies to keep me from leaving was a huge break in trust and in the illusion that I had created of what I thought this relationship was going to be. I could feel the impact on my mental health creeping in from repeat betrayals and the self-worth wound bleeding from the fact I hadn't walked away yet despite being shown he did not respect me. After all, would someone treat you this way if they valued you and if they saw you as someone worthy of being treated with love and respect? More to the point, why would I stay when I was being shown I was not valued or respected? The feeling of knowing deep down what was going on, but feeling addicted to or trapped inside the magnetic vortex of the breadcrumbs of hope he threw out was soul destroying.

He gave just enough breadcrumbs to keep me there, but not enough to feel safe and secure. I was getting just enough to give me hope things would improve and that I might be throwing away what could be my happily ever after, but not enough to allow me to trust and relax into the relationship. It was an awful and disempowering cycle to be stuck in.

My reactions intensified as he tried to justify and project the situations of betrayal onto me, making it somehow about me not seeing things right and overreacting, as he deflected the focus to my reaction as the problem and away from the actual cause of his repeat behaviour. It was a typical gaslighting technique he would use for years to come to deflect from his behaviour and have me doubting my perception and reality. Living in a state of chronic confusion within the fog he created, with the immense internal conflict because of this gaslighting, l coped by shutting down that inner sense of knowing the truth and listened to his words as gospel instead. Was I really going crazy? Are things really not as they seem? Is something deeply wrong with me to make me perceive such a situation that isn't real? He wanted me to stay after all and merely wanted me to be more reasonable and trusting. Surely he wouldn't do anything unfaithful again after the issues we have already had to date, witnessing directly how much it was hurting me, and seeing how it is damaging our relationship. I was convinced that things would be different from now on.

Not long after this, I caught him out yet again. On this occasion, he suddenly became defensive, cold, and callous. This time, he jumped in first, demanding that he wanted to end our relationship. That he realised he was still in love with his ex-girlfriend. He expressed that my trust issues were ruining us and that he couldn't help me. He just discarded me like I was nothing. I felt used and betrayed and so crippled by the pain. He didn't like being held accountable. I was no longer the beneficial narcissistic supply he needed if I was going to hold him accountable for his behaviours and set boundaries about what I would accept. Little did I know at this stage that this discard was also due to him having a glimpse of hope that he could secure supply again from his ex-girlfriend and this had become his focus.

The next couple of months that followed were dark. I didn't hear from him. I was completely discarded. My self-worth was shot. There was deep betrayal sitting within me and a feeling of despair and hopelessness after having tried everything to communicate openly, to share my expectations, to give him the opportunity to do the right thing by me when hearing what I needed and wanted at this stage in my life. I was chemically addicted to the unhealthy bond that he had created. The fluctuating surges of stress hormones that were released during the chaos and betrayals alternated with the soothing effect of the bonding hormone oxytocin that was released during the intense love bombing phase. He would declare his undying love and told me all the things I wanted to hear to feel secure in the relationship. Through my healing journey, I know now that this same biochemical concoction of stress and bonding hormones that caused the trauma bonding in this relationship was the same and familiar feeling I had experienced in my childhood.

My nervous system had gravitated to what was familiar, yet unhealthy, in my adult relationship. My nervous system recognised emotional unavailability and emotional manipulation as normal and acted in the same way in trying to seek security and safety from those who could not provide this. My system was used to experiencing emotional unavailability and love co-existing. The inconsistency and cycles of chaos and drama were all I knew and, although uncomfortable and unpleasant, I was drawn to its familiarity.

I have since reflected on all the "nice guys" that were grounded, available and reliable. The ones I felt bored with or lacked chemistry with. I realise now that my nervous system did not know calm, reliable or consistent, so this persona repelled me as it was not familiar and I always felt like there was no spark. This all occurs at a subconscious level, so until we understand and dissect our patterns and repeat experiences in life, we won't recognise this underlying neuroscience playing out in our world and causing ongoing havoc in our life.

On the outside, I was a highly independent, capable and successful woman, and this is how I felt to a certain degree. But I realised, since coming out of this experience, that this extreme independence was actually toxic independence. An unhealthy coping mechanism from never having support or a reliable person in my life and therefore the belief that it isn't safe to rely on others. That I am a burden if I have needs and that I am not worthy of asking to have my needs met by others.

Unfortunately, I hadn't had this insight drop into my conscious awareness at this stage, and a couple of months after he discarded me and ended our relationship, he suddenly made contact again and returned to my life. He declared his undying love and gave me an over-exaggerated apology and future promises of change and commitment. Despite my internal unease and resistance, I was lured into the relationship once again. I fell for the excessive love bombing, future promises and an almost non-negotiable insistence that we must be together with his claims that he was a changed man and is ready to commit now. I recall having in-depth conversations to ensure he knew what my expectations were and expressing repeatedly that I would not handle any more betrayals, as it had impacted me so much already. I should have listened to the saying: "A leopard never changes his spots."

Less than a couple of months later, I had an emotional crash after seeing evidence that after he had called our relationship off, he had flown across the country to rekindle his relationship with his ex-girlfriend, declaring his undying love for her and promising to change. Unfortunately for me, she cut him down and rejected his advances, likely having been through these similar cycles herself and having learnt.

It was her rejection that motivated him to secure a position back into my life to ensure he had a source of supply from someone he knew at the time wouldn't reject him. I was an easy target. After all, I had always been easy to manipulate before. The soul deep betrayal of discovering yet another time that he was playing me and literally using my heart as a falling pad led to what I can only describe as a mini emotional breakdown. I was dysregulated. I was literally pulling my hair out. How could he do this? How could he be so dishonest, declare his love, and use me the way he did?

I reacted big. I called it off for good, or so I thought. I didn't want to hear from him. My pulling away made him try even harder to lure me back in. All the words, all the promises, the lavish gifts, the fake tears, and telling me he would support me in my dreams. That he wanted children with me and to start a life together. I still held firm and said, enough is enough. I had wasted enough time. I was done. I wanted to move forward with my life.

This loss of control he now had over me, and my staunch resistance to not letting him back into my life this time, triggered something intensely within him and unbeknown to me, he began the escalation of his strategic plan to get me back under his control and be the supply he needed me to be. A few days later, after cutting contact with him so I could have some space to recover and move on, he turned up on my doorstep, with his bags on Christmas Day, declaring his love and stating he wasn't letting me go and was moving in and not going home. He affirmed, as if in some grand gesture of generosity, that he was giving up his own life to move up to be with me. He then told me he had already arranged a job transfer, cancelled the lease on his home and had no other option now but to move in with me, into the house that I owned. Considering we lived in different states and it was Christmas Day, this seemed a very dramatic statement and commitment. Or it was irrational, controlling and erratic behaviour that I would see repeated over the upcoming years. There is a saying that goes, *"No-one falls in love faster than a narcissist who needs somewhere to live"*.

It couldn't have been truer in this case. I knew deep down it was strange to force yourself into someone's life in this way after they had told you no. I desperately wanted it to be real and genuine, and he was incredibly convincing.

I reached out to my then best friend and voiced the situation and my confusion. Of course, she already knew. He had been grooming her since we met and had recently liaised with her about his plan, planting the seed that what he was doing was a romantic gesture of deep commitment to me. She fell for it and encouraged him and confirmed with me she thought it was such a lovely gesture and shows his true desire to commit. Being so influenced by this friend in this phase of life, I listened to her and squashed down my inner knowing that something wasn't right.

I tried to embrace this "romantic" gesture and held onto the illusion that this time it would be different. If only I saw the patterns clearly. If only I trusted my intuition. If only I looked at past behaviour instead of listening to his words again. This was a true sliding doors moment and the beginning of the end of my world as I knew it.

"Words not matching actions is called manipulation. And refusing to be held accountable for it is called gaslighting."
Unknown Author.

CHAPTER 4

IF YOU ARE NOT OKAY, I AM NOT OKAY

I realise now that I allowed this dysfunctional behaviour because of low self-worth and the core belief that I wasn't worthy of love and respect, stemming from childhood. Through my lifelong journey of self-development, personal healing and my training in trauma informed mental health, I gained clarity on the behaviours and patterns I portrayed that originated from an insecure attachment wounding. I recognised I flipped from a sometimes anxious attachment to a sometimes avoidant attachment. This is known as a Disorganised Attachment Style. I was constantly seeking ways to feel safe in my relationships. One coping mechanism in particular that I adopted, and it became a strong personality trait, was "people pleasing". The sacrifice of my own needs to avoid rejection, abuse or abandonment from others. People pleasing is a trauma response from childhood and the resulting belief is that to be safe and avoid rejection or abuse, you need to abandon your authentic self, betray your own needs, and appease or please others. It is the pattern of trying to be who others expect you or demand you be and results in deep self-abandonment and betrayal of self.

This dynamic I had entered felt familiar and aligned with the emotional climate I grew up in, and although not healthy, it was all I knew. I see now I was experiencing impacts of unresolved trauma from my earlier years and I had developed a co-dependant way to be safe and avoid rejection and abandonment.

Co-dependency is a kind of dysfunctional dynamic where one person sacrifices their needs and true desires to caretake, rescue and enable their partners unhealthy behaviour, to avoid upsetting them or losing the connection. It is the unbalanced power dynamic of one person being a giver and the other taking advantage in a self-serving way. This way of being I lived by stemmed from an insecure attachment and associated low self-worth because of the absence of emotional attunement and a secure attachment to my caregiver. The associated behaviour of sacrificing my true needs to please others resulted from the underlying belief that I was not worthy of love for who I was. At a surface level, it was a feeling that if they were not okay, then I was not okay. That I am not safe in the connection if they demonstrate signs of being upset, bored or displeased. This resulted in the need for me to always give my ex-partner what he wanted to be happy at the detriment of myself.

A person with co-dependent coping mechanisms has an unbalanced need to give. A narcissist has a strong sense of entitlement to take. This dynamic between the two is like a magnet. Both stem from childhood trauma and a deep lack of self-identity and self-worth, but the coping mechanisms in both are very different. Someone with co-dependent coping mechanisms has the underlying intention of seeking safety and harmony in the dynamic. A narcissist, however, has the underlying intention of manipulating and exploiting for self-gain. Co-dependency soothes the self-worth wound by developing a need to give and please to feel valued and worthy of the relationship. Narcissism soothes this wounded part by living through the ego and developing a sense of entitlement while expecting others to meet their every need, please them and give to them. These polarities are like light and dark and attract to each other like a magnet.

Co-dependency has us using people as a mirror. For co-dependency to develop, we would typically have grown up in an environment where we didn't feel seen, didn't feel appreciated, and didn't feel loved in the way we needed. There may have also been elements of not feeling a safe connection with a caregiver or experiences that left us feeling abandoned, whether physically or emotionally. We don't develop a core self or a strong sense of self, and we don't get to know ourselves or develop healthy self-worth. We don't get to truly see ourselves. It's a parents' responsibility to reflect to us as children how amazing we are, how beautiful we are, how valued we are and how loved we are… just for being ourselves. When we don't get that reflection back, we end up craving to be seen and accepted by other people. We end up seeking to be told who we are and receiving validation for our worth by other people, in particular in our intimate relationships. Therefore, people with co-dependent coping mechanisms will often go into roles where they fix, rescue or over give, so that they can be seen through other people's eyes as good. It's so important to become aware and acknowledge this wounding and realise that the only way that you are going to heal this is by becoming your OWN mirror, that reflects back to YOURSELF just how amazing you truly are. When you truly believe this at a core level, your life will transform. It's about the healing of self-worth and establishing a strong sense of self so you know deep down who you truly are, that you are innately good just for being you, and that you always have been enough. The need to be seen and validated by a partner will no longer exist and therefore toxic and, in particular, narcissistic relationships, will be a thing of your past.

As we recognise co-dependency in ourselves and our relationship, it is important to recognise it is not our fault. It is equally important to step into radical accountability and take full personal responsibility for our role in our own healing and recovery. Going inward and looking at the rejected and disowned parts of ourself, and doing our shadow work for our own healing, is essential in shifting this pattern of behaviour to break the cycle of unhealthy relationships. There is absolutely a time for self-validation and for sitting in the resulting emotion from the experiences that have very much happened to us. There also comes a time, when we are ready, to move into radical personal accountability and take action to do what is needed to heal those unhealed parts of us that have kept us stuck in dysfunctional cycles. This is where our personal power lies. This is where the key to our freedom and happiness resides.

CHAPTER 5

ENTRAPMENT

I had suddenly gone from living a life of freedom on my own with my two dogs and a housemate who I rented a room out to assist me with my mortgage. I was working full time and living a clean and healthy life. I had little drama in my world and was suddenly thrown into a full-blown, live-in de facto relationship with someone I had recently walked away from. It was intense, confusing, like I didn't have a say in the matter, yet at another level it was also exciting, hopeful and the outcome I had dreamed of from a loyal, compatible, caring, supportive and committed partner he was affirming he was going to be. These critical aspects were the vital yet absent pieces of the puzzle that would be the unravelling of not only the relationship in years to come, but of my entire life.

A couple of days after he moved into my home and placed himself in the centre of my world, he took it upon himself to tell my housemate he had to move out as we needed our own space. I remember cringing at this and feeling as if I was being taken over by the dominance of the "husband" I had gained overnight. I tried to voice my concerns about how I needed my housemate for the contribution to my mortgage payments and that's why I had someone in the first place, as well as the awkwardness of discarding someone who I had committed to providing a long-term space for them to live. It felt selfish and insensitive to just kick them out so suddenly. Not to him however, it was like it was an entitlement or right he had since he was now the man of this household. Not wanting to cause issues for our new relationship, I let it go.

I assumed he would naturally contribute with rent or expenses of some sort, knowing the impact of losing my housemate was going to have on my ability to cover my mortgage; wrong once again. After a couple of months and the increasing strain on my financial situation with covering all the costs of our living expenses, I had to say something to him or I was going to go under financially. On raising my concern about how he had moved in, kicked my housemate out and after a couple of months I'm left struggling to cover all expenses for the both of us, he acted surprised as if it had completely slipped his mind, and he instantly said he would rectify and contribute to our living expenses. I felt uncomfortable asking and believed that he genuinely just forgot and had gotten caught up in the busyness of his new life.

We got stuck into life. It was busy. Full of action and adventures. I took up cycling with him. We would go out for dinners, and we spent weekends at the beach or camping. We trained and exercised together. We socialised a lot. We also drank more frequently than I ever had before. He worked away interstate during the week and came home on weekends. Our weekends together were always jammed packed full of activities. He needed to be doing something all the time, and I got caught up with always ensuring we had something planned so he wouldn't get bored and lose interest in me or our life together.

Although it was fun, I mentioned I felt like we only bonded over activities. I raised my concerns about what would happen if we didn't do all the fun and exciting things together. How would he be? How would he cope if we had children and life changed to a more mundane routine? He affirmed to me it was more than just activities and told me it was just my unfounded insecurities creeping in. His words were always so convincing and were what I wanted to hear, so it was easy to just believe and accept them.

After a few months of my new and action packed life, I felt completely exhausted and burnt out. I thought there was something wrong with my health, so I went and had some tests done. All came back clear. The exhaustion and fatigue continued. I raised this with him and explained I think I needed to have more downtime and less alcohol in my life. Before he moved in, I was vibrant, healthy and energised, and now I was feeling depleted and exhausted most of the time. He seemed to acknowledge this during our conversation, yet life carried on the same with no change.

His consumption of alcohol every day that we spent together would become a big issue for me. I had to raise it again and explained once again that I highly valued health and that drinking every day in my home didn't align with my values or the life I wanted to live. He insisted he was just caught up in the excitement of our new relationship and living together and that it wasn't normal for him. I took this as comfort that the drinking would reduce and things would change to something more acceptable in this area. The drinking habits did not cease, and this particular misaligned lifestyle habit would become another of the major areas of conflict in our life for the remaining years of our relationship. The drinking never ceased. The arguments around this over the years escalated. The impacts of his behaviour while drinking were to become some of the most traumatic experiences of my life and some of the most dangerous situations I would be caught in within my own home.

Moving forward nine months, we became engaged to be married. How this came about was typical of the erratic and impulsive behaviour he would prove to show repeatedly over the years that followed. However, I was caught up in needing to move forward with securing our commitment, as it felt we were too far in and in too deep to go back the other way now. The only way was forward. I was determined to make this work. I just had to make sure I was who he needed me to be to ensure he stayed interested and committed. A dysfunctional thought pattern and belief I had carried my entire life. *If I can be better or who they need me to be, it will ensure their love and commitment, and I will avoid rejection or abandonment.* It was a life lesson that I was soon to become awaken to that was not a reality and this self-sacrifice of my authentic self and my needs was not the way to establish safety in relationships.

On reflection, I adopted this in my friendships, my family of origin interactions and even in my work, in which I was always very successful and well respected. The art of reading and being highly attuned to what others want, need and expect from you and doing just that. A chronic form of self-sacrifice and self-betrayal is adopted as a personality trait and formed in childhood to stay safe and seek connections with those close to me.

We went camping one weekend around this time with some of my immediate and extended family. My ex-partner proposed to me during this trip, which was also the grand final weekend for the football which he was very passionate about. My reaction to the proposal surprised me. It also concerned me. At the moment he pulled out the ring and popped those four words, I felt myself freeze up and feel nothing but pure dread. It was only for a split second and I could push it aside and convince myself that this was exciting and something I had always wanted. I said yes and in a somewhat shocked state, we went back to the group we were camping with and shared our news. What I observed next and moving forward in my ex-partner was something I would come to realise was his core driver for almost everything he does in his life. It was the obsession with the attention he was receiving from the proposal that seemed to be his excitement. I couldn't shake the feeling that this had little to do with his love or commitment to me as a person. I disregarded this feeling and tried to join in on the excitement. For the hours that followed our engagement moment, he sat glued to his phone, watching for all the comments, communication and attention he was getting for the news he had posted out to his network. The messages and phone calls were coming in thick and fast and he was obviously in his element. I couldn't help but feel flat and almost hurt that what was supposed to be such an intimate and special day for us seemed to be about him and the attention he could gain from others. If he really knew me, he would have known that my dream situation would have been to get engaged in private with just us, and to share closeness and connectedness about our future as a couple.

It seemed the plan he had for proposing on a weekend we were away, surrounded by other people, was because he wanted to have his need for attention met by having others around. Within hours of our engagement, he was off to the pub with the boys to watch the footy finals. The following day, he was off to the pub again for the next round of finals. I felt like this engagement had nothing to do with me or our commitment but was more for the attention it was bringing him.

On the way home from our camping and engagement weekend and feeling like we had barely spent any time together, he announced he was heading interstate for work early the following morning and would then go straight to visit interstate friends on the following weekend to celebrate our engagement with them, then return to his interstate work straight from there the week after. So, I was sitting there feeling completely disconnected from him and flat from our engagement, that seemed to be very little about me or us. I raised my concerns about the fact we were newly engaged and had barely spent quality time together to enjoy it, and that he was going away for the next two weeks with a trip in there to celebrate our engagement with his mates without me even there. It seemed odd, and it was very hurtful. He didn't like that I had those views and argued he wanted to be there with his mates and that's what he was doing. I cried myself to sleep that night after he was asleep. Something wasn't right. I thought things would change once he decided to fully commit like this.

Two weeks later, when he came home, and I finally saw him for the first time since our engagement weekend, he shared that one of his best friends had also just announced their engagement. He said it with such irritation and with an almost disappointed tone. When asking him about why he seems so disappointed, he sighed and said it just seems like everyone has forgotten about our news and our engagement and it's all about them now. I challenged him on this and asked, aren't you happy for your friend? He got slightly defensive and brushed it off and said, "yes, of course I am," and changed the subject and walked away.

It left me sitting there, quite stunned. I realised that he really was caught up in our engagement, bringing him attention. It really had nothing to do with me or us. It really irritated him for the rest of the day. It was like he was battling internally with the fact this huge news that he thought was going to give him ongoing attention for the whole time until our actual wedding was suddenly not interesting.

Time continued on and through the planning, I felt glimpses of excitement and got caught up in the experience. I had asked my three sisters to be my bridesmaids. I really wanted it to be special for them. I thought this was an opportunity to bring us closer together. I thought they'd be so honoured and so excited to stand next to me on my special day. My younger sister had actually gotten engaged approximately six months prior. I thought this was going to be the most amazing year with two family weddings in the same year.

Little did I know that behind the scenes was a dark festering of insecurity and resentment building up from my younger sister, who was supported by my mother and the rest of my sisters. What I thought was a beautiful and amazing year for our family was actually a year that was going to tear down the already fragile structure of our family unit and, in particular, my place within it.

My sister and I both continued with planning our weddings. They were very different weddings, and that was completely fine, as far as I was concerned. I was caught up in my planning and was excited and happy for my sister for her wedding and her planning. I noticed strange behaviours creeping in from my mother and my sisters and I thought I must be misinterpreting things at first, so I disregarded it, brushed it away and just continued on. It then became more and more clear that something wasn't right. Something was going on behind the scenes, but I couldn't quite put my finger on it. It was almost like they were trying to intentionally ignore me and take little, in fact, no interest in my upcoming wedding, which surprised me and also concerned me because they were my bridesmaids and I obviously needed their input and their interaction with the planning. I felt really hurt. I didn't know what was going on.

I arranged a beautiful day with a champagne breakfast for my sister and my mother to include them in helping me find my wedding dress. On this day, my mother spent the entire day talking to my sister about her wedding and her dress and hardly took any interest in my planning, despite this being a special day arranged to go shopping for my wedding dress. She was over the top in trying to convert the focus to my sister. When I asked my mother if she'd like to look for a dress for her mother of the bride's outfit and she simply said to me,

"I not talking about your wedding until your sisters is done."

This was a complete shutdown and, considering we were on a special day to look for my wedding dress, I felt very hurt and very confused. I just didn't understand what was going on. Something that was supposed to be such a huge milestone in my wedding planning and such a special day ended up being so tainted. I left this day feeling really confused and hurt. I wanted my family to be happy for me. I wanted them to be involved, and I wanted them to be a part of my special day. There had been no communication or conversations to explain anything to me, so I was left very confused and hurt by the unexplained treatment towards me.

Shortly after this time, I was speaking to my mother on the phone while I was at work one afternoon. I excitedly mentioned that my best friend was planning my hen's day. My mother suddenly turned on me and snapped at me, stating that I shouldn't have booked my wedding in the same year as my sister, and that I was taking her limelight. I was shocked. It completely caught me off guard. I didn't understand. These were two completely separate weddings, so how could I be taking her limelight? There's more than enough space in one family for two weddings. The more I expressed myself to my mother about how I didn't understand and how much it hurt to have her favour my sister and try to drag me down and taint my experience to make my sister feel better about her insecurities, the more she turned on me and the conversation blew up into a full-blown argument about how selfish I was. It ended with me being told I should have known and that I should never have booked my wedding in the same year as my sister. I was told if I insisted on having my wedding that year and wouldn't cancel it, then I would have to deal with my family, ignoring me. I left work in tears and called my ex-partner. He told me not to worry and that it would all blow over. He couldn't have been more wrong.

Leading up to our wedding, my sisters and mother all turned on me and expected me to stay silent. They would not engage in discussions or focus on my upcoming wedding until my sister's special day was over. Considering they were my bridesmaids, this was a difficult demand to accept. My ex-partner tried to get himself in the middle of the situation to manipulate them into the outcome he wanted. When he realised my family had already cut me out and were punishing me for what they saw as me causing my sister to feel inadequate and insecure, he stopped trying to manipulate them and he turned on me.

He basically gave me an ultimatum to fix things with my family or he was going to leave me, call off the wedding and move back interstate where he had come from. He claimed he was bringing me a whole family from his side and said I was now bringing him nothing. This was a dark and deeply traumatic time for me. Every waking moment felt like torture. I couldn't escape the reality of what was happening. My family had already banded together and kept me squashed down, silenced, and without a voice. I either accepted the blame that I was this awful and selfish person for daring to book my wedding in the same year as my sister and cancel everything or accept the consequences of having them ignore me. I tried to justify, explain how I felt and my reasons, but I was continually ganged up on and bullied relentlessly.

When my family realised that others outside the family didn't see the issues with two family weddings occurring in the same year, they changed the narrative to make out the issue was about my character, about me being inherently bad since childhood. It was like they had to fabricate a narrative that justified why they were pushing me out. This continued on until our permanent estrangement in the year that followed my wedding.

My ex-partner and I ended up having couples counselling around this issue and the counsellor was supportive of my view in that he was supposed to be marrying me for me, and not for what I could bring to him. We spoke about what it means to be a supportive partner and that when you grow up and marry you become your own family unit. He couldn't resonate with that, and he continued to struggle with the fact I couldn't just make my family act differently and fix it. This disconnect went on for months, leading up to our wedding.

Six weeks prior to our big day, and with our relationship in turmoil, I tried to call the wedding off. He became enraged. He was furious and commented, "what would everyone think if we called off the wedding now?"

He was merely concerned about his image. I faced the sudden loss of my family through the betrayal and relentless bullying that I hadn't seen coming, followed by a fiancé that clearly wasn't marrying me for me, but for the external life he thought I was going to provide for him.

I have done many years of soul searching, therapy, and self-reflection to understand how this came to be. Becoming a mother myself has shown me that there is dysfunction in my family of origin for this outcome to occur. Healthy parents who love their children unconditionally, who are emotionally mature, and have the capacity to be accountable for their own feelings and behaviours without projection, triangulating or playing siblings against each other, will not be motivated or even capable of betraying or discarding one of their children. As a mother, all I know is that I would never become estranged by choice from a biological child. There is nothing they could do or say that would ever make me turn my back on them, betray them, or stop loving them. Am I the perfect parent at all times? No, certainly not. Do I feel frustrated and take my stress out on my children sometimes? Yes, for sure. What I know to be certain, however, is that my intentions and desire is always to be the best mother I can be for them, and I know without a doubt that they feel loved unconditionally by me. I would never abandon them or stop loving them because they challenge me or highlight my own shortfalls. I firmly believe our children are our greatest teachers if we have the courage to allow them to be our mirror, without projecting back onto them. I also cannot deny that they, even at their young ages, call me out and hold me accountable. When I know deep down I have let my own fears come out in unhealthy ways to protect them or have let my stress spill out into my interactions with them, and as uncomfortable as it is sometimes when they call me out, it is always welcomed and acknowledged. We have open and vulnerable discussions and I apologise to them often. I try every day to hold myself accountable, apologise when needed and make a genuine effort to change any behaviour that isn't supportive of their healthy growth and development. I allow my children to have a voice and be heard despite their age. I hold firm boundaries with them when needed, and they are guided to take personal accountability for their choices and behaviours, but this also applies to me as their mother. If I say or do something that they believe or see as not good for their needs and they express this to me, I listen. I acknowledge and I take action to either explain the reasoning or do things differently next time if warranted. These are some of the reasons I know I am on the path to breaking generational dysfunction, as having a parent be accountable and own their behaviour, and being seen, heard and acknowledged for my feelings and needs, was something I never experienced in my childhood. This carried on well into adulthood where I was expected to keep silent to dysfunction and if I called out behaviour, I was shunned, ganged up on and eventually ostracised completely. I know that this is already different for my own children and the ripple effect of this on future generations is profound and life changing.

CHAPTER 6

GENERATIONAL TRAUMA

It takes courage to step away from the familiar, find your strength, and walk your own path.

I came from a family of four female siblings, all close in age. My father, who has since passed, was disconnected from himself and emotionally unavailable, although a very gentle and intelligent man who I feel nothing but love and compassion for. I don't recall a single occasion in my entire childhood where he raised his voice to me or my siblings and there was always such a passiveness about him. He lost his own father as a teenager who I understand had undiagnosed post-traumatic stress disorder from World War II and who suffered from substance abuse issues. I don't know much about my father's childhood, but I have learned through my study in trauma and mental health, that my father was dissociated and disconnected from himself. He didn't know how to feel, express or process emotions, so was highly suppressed and repressed. He could not connect deeply with or attune emotionally to others, including his own children. He had such a kindness and gentleness to his nature and a highly intelligent mind. This was combined with an inability to express or articulate emotions, or hold space for and connect with the feelings of others.

My mother was carrying her own unhealed trauma and unhealthy conditioning from her childhood. Her trauma had caused her to become emotionally stunted, lacking emotional maturity and wisdom. She could not model healthy emotional regulation, conflict resolution or self-confidence and therefore passed on significant dysfunctional patterns, conditioning and generational trauma to the family unit. When her needs were not met or her way was not cooperated with, her coping mechanism was to covertly manipulate, to gain what she wanted or to inflict punishments when she felt she lacked control. Withdrawing of love, silent treatment, favouring attention towards those who complied with her desires and passive aggressiveness were common behaviours shown within the home environment. This reflected a grown woman with a wounded inner child who also never felt seen and valued and, as a coping mechanism, developed dysfunctional behaviours to avoid the shame and projecting the rage she felt inside onto others, in particular her own children. She had a passive aggressive bitterness towards her own parents and she could never heal these wounds before they died. Even in their death, she displayed resentment towards them, and although there was no active conflict, she did not attend their funerals.

I recall a huge fracture that was created between my mother and myself during my father's last months. I was visiting my parents and went out on a walk with my mother and while she often used me as a sounding board for her adult feelings and problems, her venting and emotional dumping onto me was too much for me to carry and was an inappropriate reversal of the parent child relationship. I was twenty-one years old. She would complain to me about my father. He was so unwell and spent much of his time in bed exhausted with chronic pain in his last months. He had been given a terminal diagnosis and there was nothing that could be done to treat his condition. My father did not have the capacity to give my mother excessive attention or meet her needs as he was deeply depressed, knowing he was dying and was just focused on trying to get through each day.

During this walk, my mother vented to me about my unwell dad, to the point of aggressively stating she wished, "he would just hurry up and die". This was my father. I was struggling to process the realisation that he was dying, and to have my mother tell me directly she wished he would just hurry up and die was too much for me to hold and carry. I shut down and felt immense grief at hearing this from my mother, but said nothing. I watched on during this visit as she treated my dad like absolute rubbish in his dying days. I could see how much pain and anguish he was in, completely alone and unsupported. One evening, I logged onto the family computer in the home to find a webpage open for a support chat group that showed he had been reaching out to strangers about his condition and the struggle he was having in accepting his fate. It was the first time I had ever witnessed my father express any sort of vulnerability. It was heartbreaking to read of the distress he was in and how unsupported and alone he was feeling. I didn't have the skills or capacity to address this with him, so I said nothing. I continued to observe my mother's lack of compassion towards him, and I continued to suppress the impact this had on me.

She could not put herself in his shoes and feel empathy for his experience. Her inner child was demanding attention, perceiving the situation to be all about her and playing the role of the victim in the circumstances. He ended up dying alone in a hospital in another town. We discovered later that he had requested a *not for resuscitation* order. He very much wanted to die in the end. He was so alone, and my mother was simply awful to him by projecting her own resentment and bitterness.

I didn't realise, but I held onto this resentment towards my mother for what I witnessed in my dad's dying days. I saw her for who she really was and I lost respect for her and didn't feel safe in that she was a trustworthy person who had her children's or others' best interest at heart. I could block it out over the years that followed and had nice interactions with her, but I was always closed off and I never showed my true self or felt safe to show any vulnerability. I kept her at arm's length. If I'm honest, I'd felt this way most of my life, but this really consolidated in early adulthood.

Now that I have progressed on my healing journey and emotional maturity, I can see she was acting from her unhealed trauma. She was stuck in the emotional age of a child who was trying to have her needs met. It was the only way she knew how to address her own pain and fears of the future, and I have compassion for that now.

As her daughter, I noticed the deep sense of shame and lack of confidence my mother had regarding what other people thought of her. This feeling was projected onto her children, though I can only speak from my experience. I often experienced episodes of emotional dysregulation directed towards me as a child and I recall one occasion in particular that had a tremendous impact on my life and sense of self. I was five years old, and we had only recently moved interstate, away from our extended family and the life we knew. I was playing around boisterously in the kitchen of our rental home while my mother was baking. I specifically remember this hideous brown carpet that was throughout the house, including the kitchen floor. In my typical energetic way, I was bouncing around the kitchen playing and although I don't recall, I assume I was probably told multiple times to settle down. Then I somehow knocked over a bottle of red food colouring onto the kitchen carpet. It went everywhere. Next thing, I was being screamed at and hit multiple times. Complete and utter dysregulation directed towards my five-year-old self who didn't see it coming. It sent me into such a state of shock that ruptured whatever small bond or sense of safety in the connection with my mother that may have existed.

The words she screamed at me are forever etched in my soul and fractured a piece of me I could never retrieve. She bellowed at me with such rawness and rage, "Get out! I never want to see you ever again! Get out of here and don't ever come back!", as she literally belted me out the door. I still remember the terror and immense hurt as I ran, and I ran up the road and away from home, trembling from head to toe, tears streaming down my face.

We lived across the road from a large industrial factory full of hundreds of tradesmen. I ran across the road to the factory and hid behind a brick wall. As I sat crouched down, I was holding onto hope my mother would soon come looking for me. I waited in anticipation for the moment she would walk across and find me, reconnect and everything would be ok. That moment never came. She never came. No one came. When I realised no-one was coming, I began my plan about where I was going to run away to. It was frightening. I had no-where to go, and I wasn't wanted at home.

THE DEPTH OF HER SURVIVAL

After what felt like hours of my running away, I was tired and out of survival, I timidly made my way back home. I remember the fear, insecurity and shame I felt about walking back into the home and seeing my mother. It shut me down. I was afraid of being rejected. As a five-year-old, I took those words literally.

There were no other safe adults in my life for me to reach out to. I did not have a bond with any other adults as we had moved away from our extended family, and I had nowhere to go. When I re-entered the home, my mother acted as if nothing had happened and gave me the silent treatment. No one had noticed I was gone. No one asked where I'd been. There was no debrief of what had occurred and no repair of the shattering words bellowed at me only hours before.

My self-worth and the health of my nervous system were paved through one experience like this after another in my early childhood, and I soon developed a core personality trait of people pleasing. Losing my authentic self to maintain connection and avoiding rejection by sacrificing my own opinions and needs to please others. I would often get praised at school, in the shopping centres and by family friends about what a quiet and good girl I was, as did my siblings at a young age. We were there to be an extension of our mother and if we made her look bad to others through our behaviour, it brought up her insecurities and immense fear about what others thought of her; so we were moulded to be perfect, not inconvenience others and keep quiet. This helped my mother feel like she was seen as a good mother by others as she linked our perfect behaviour to be a reflection of her worth. The fear of making a mistake, being too loud, daring to ask for anything or messing up became a chronic hypervigilance within me to always be aware of the moods and signs from others, that may indicate they disapproved of me or were getting upset.

There were other obvious causes that pushed me to live in survival mode at a young age. I recall being criticised and shamed in front of my siblings and teased for not letting my mother cuddle or hug me as a young child. It was communicated as if there was something inherently wrong with me for behaving that way. As a young child, I apparently used to stand stiff with my arms straight by my side and wouldn't return an embrace or hug. I know now that I was completely frozen and didn't feel safe in my connections in the home.

When I was eleven years old, I remember feeling so hurt and distraught as jokes were made about me at the dinner table with my mother often stating publicly that she wanted to get me tested for autism when I was younger as she thought I was autistic because I didn't show affection to her along with other related traits.

They often turned me into the family scapegoat. Early in my teenage years, I was body shamed by my mother and one of my sisters followed this lead to project her own pain and insecurities onto me. It was a learnt behaviour to use me as a punching bag. I distinctively remember my mother taking food straight off my plate on occasions and putting it onto my sister's plate at the dinner table. When my sister would complain and question why I didn't have to eat as much as she did, my mother would state right in front of me that I didn't need it as I was heavy enough, big-boned and didn't need to be fattened up like my sister did. I remember holding back tears and feeling frozen, trying to pretend the criticism didn't deeply hurt me. As the years went on, I shut down even more and tried to search for my own connections outside of the home. This was seen as rebellion and to this day, I am held in purgatory for my teenage years for behaviours that stemmed from attempting to seek acceptance, connection, identity and a sense of belonging in the world.

THE DEPTH OF HER SURVIVAL

I feel uncomfortable sharing the truth about my family and I am limited in what I can share out of respect for them, so I will leave it with these few examples to give an insight into how childhood experiences can pave the way for survival mechanisms in personality and life patterns in adulthood. I have felt quite conflicted over the past years as I understand and feel compassion for my parents and how they were with an awareness that they did the best within the capacity of their own unresolved trauma. They were not conscious of their own trauma to do the work and break the cycles for their own children. It saddens me to think of what must be immense shame and pain being carried internally to feel the only option is to turn on your own child, rather than face the fear of personal accountability. I have forgiven my mother and I simply feel neutral now. No significant feelings of love, yet also no significant resentment or bitterness. It's simply an acceptance that this was my journey to experience and to be given the opportunity, lessons, and wisdom to work towards breaking generational cycles of dysfunction for my own children. I would not have a conscious awareness of the dysfunction and conditioning of my upbringing had I not had the suffering and heartache to wake me up to the trauma I needed to heal. And I would likely have parented my own children with the same limiting beliefs, unhealthy conditioning and unconscious coping mechanisms, without having lived through these deeply traumatic and life changing experiences.

Now that I am a mother myself and know that there is nothing my children could ever do that would make me turn my back on them or stop loving them, I can somewhat reframe this experience and see my mother through a lens of compassion for the depth of pain, insecurity and trauma that must be carried for a mother to betray and discard a child of their own. My own children understand who their grandmother is but don't know her and we don't talk much about her unless they ask curious questions. I don't believe there is much hope or benefit in trying to reconnect in this lifetime and sometimes it is healthier to let go and create your own family, your chosen family, who can love you unconditionally, have aligned values, who see and accept you for who you really are and who feel safe to your nervous system.

In adulthood, I had a reasonable relationship with my family, but always felt drained after spending too much time with them. I also felt different and like I couldn't truly be myself. It wasn't safe to be vulnerable and make mistakes, judgement was always an undertone and shining too brightly was met with being put down. My entire value system was completely different to theirs, despite coming from the same family. On the surface and to the outside world, they projected an image of being very sweet and polite individuals and behaved in a way that was always acceptable.

Behind closed doors, the undertone within the relationship dynamic was a very different picture and the way they banded together to protect the family image is very similar to what I married into in my in-law family. Some could say, and I'm sure they have said, that I'm the common denominator to the issues with my family of origin and my in-law family that followed, so I must be the problem. My old self would have been crippled with insecurity and fear of judgement around this. The progressively healed version of me these days knows with clarity what I have experienced and the dynamics at play that I was born into and ultimately married into.

In a dysfunctional family system, the healthiest person or the one who thinks and operates outside of the family group often causes friction. They create resistance in the family dynamics and other members become uncomfortable and triggered, therefore coping by attempting to silence, scapegoat or project shortfalls onto the family member who is different or speaks up. It's important to understand if you can relate to this type of dynamic, that you being treated as if you are unlovable and as if there is something wrong with you for being different to them, is about their dysfunctional vision, and nothing to do with your value.

Family Systems Therapy (FST), developed by psychiatrist Murray Bowen in the 1950s, refers to dysfunctional family units as having what is called an "Identified Patient". A dysfunctional family unit sacrifices a member and places them in the role of Identified Patient, or Scapegoat. This allows the rest of the family unit to remain blameless, to be able to see themselves as good people, parents and siblings. By targeting and labelling one member as the sick or troubled one, the rest of the family unit can avoid accountability, completely absolve themselves of any responsibility and avoid feeling the deep shame of acknowledging their part in the dysfunction. Often the Identified Patient will eventually develop unhealthy coping mechanisms or mental health symptoms from bearing the load and blame of the family dysfunction. This can present in the way of addictions, anxiety, depression, emotional reactiveness, suicidal ideation or acts of rebellion. They are often labelled as being mentally unstable by the family unit and ultimately driven to this fate while they remain a part of the family dynamic. Often the child singled out for the role of Identified Patient is the most emotionally healthy, most cognitively aware, most sensitive and intuitive and the most balanced member of the household. The Identified Patient is often pointed to by the family unit as the source of all the family problems and conflict, instead of looking at the family system itself and the environment as flawed. This typically develops when an unhealthy family system unconsciously outsources and projects its dysfunction onto this individual member. This can sometimes be directed towards the family member who is a perceived risk for exposing or shining a light on the family dysfunction. The principles behind FST are based on the understanding that when one member of a family unit presents with mental health or behavioural symptoms and is pushed forward by the family unit as being the problem person in the family and indicating they need therapy, it is always related to the broader environment of the family itself, and little to do with the individual being inherently flawed or bad. It is always about the family system being dysfunctional that creates symptoms in an individual member who is usually put in that role unconsciously by the dysfunctional family to avoid having to acknowledge or have accountability for the unhealthy dynamic they are a part of. This is common in families where there is a parent who displays personality disorders.

We seek adult relationships that mirror what we haven't healed from in childhood, and we gravitate to that which is familiar, as an unconscious attempt to gain what we have been seeking our whole life. I have stepped away from my family of origin, and if I'm honest, they ostracised me after I attempted to speak about the dysfunction and finally stood up for myself. I was unwilling to play the role that kept me safe in these dynamics, so more conflict arose and they pushed me to the outer. I am no longer prepared to have to make myself small, to be silenced, to play the role of scapegoat and fit in a box to make others feel more comfortable in their own skin.

I now know that difficult conversations are healthy and mutual personal accountability is a must for healthy relationships to thrive. I was the scapegoat of my family of origin and my ex-partner observed this dynamic and used these vulnerabilities to his advantage when I left our marriage. As I held him accountable to his abuse during the later years of our relationship, he placed me in and encouraged his own family to have me in the scapegoat role. The dynamic, behaviours and experience were almost identical to that which I experienced in my family of origin.

I recall an occasion late one night, when my ex-partner came home drunk and physically assaulted me. He immediately rang his mother in a panic, who lived interstate, and told her what had occurred. His mother was very aware of the facts of this event and in the weeks that followed, after I insisted my ex-partner move out, his mother began calling me, trying to encourage me to let him move back in. She relayed he learnt these behaviours from his father and not her, and that she was so ashamed about what he had done. She also admitted that she had been on the receiving end of a physical altercation with my ex-partner's father, so said she understood what it's like. She continued to call me, telling me I needed to give him another chance and let him move back in. The disturbing part about this situation was that a few years later, when I finally left him for good and we officially separated, his mother completely turned on me and denied that these events ever happened or that she had ever heard anything. Gaslighting to the most severe level.

She called me early in our separation period when she realised I would not take her son back, telling me I was mentally unstable, that she had never heard of any abuse from her son towards me and attempted to intimidate me by saying that she would speak up in court claiming I had in fact physically harmed my own children. An utter distortion and reversal of the facts of the past occurrences in our relationship clearly aimed at deflecting away from her son's past behaviours. I completely lost it on the phone at these false claims that were designed to intimidate me, destabilise me and push me into silence. I was utterly distraught. It was a complete twist of events to change the narrative to paint me as unstable, abusive and her son as a victim. In the same conversation, she cruelly stated that *my own mother doesn't even love me and that I have no one in my life.*

My experience with this woman is that she demonstrated behaviours of a vindictive and callous human being who contributed to her son developing the same traits and a complete lack of empathy for others. She never once, in my experience in this family, attempted to hold her son accountable for his behaviour and continued to enable and cover for him. She saw his behaviour as a reflection of her, so had to deny and avoid acknowledging this and ultimately cover up to protect her own image. This passed on the generational dysfunction. This psychological abuse as gaslighting, intimidation, and false allegations continued with a vengeance for the next couple of years during our separation.

These traits and behaviours have since been explained to me by professionals I have sought counselling and support from, as being textbook narcissistic. They counselled me that there was nothing I could do or say to such disordered people that would ever make them suddenly feel empathy or develop the desire to do the right thing by their grandchildren.

I still to this day send photos and videos to these grandparents of our children nearly every week, and although this has been occurring for a long while now without a single response, I figured that at least I can hold my head high knowing I tried everything to encourage a relationship with their grandchildren and to give them an opportunity to put their grandchildren's wellbeing first.

THE DEPTH OF HER SURVIVAL

Deep down, I know they are not a positive influence on our children. I know they would cause more damage than good to our children's self-esteem and value system, but it is so sad to see our children have no grandparents in their life. The idea of this keeps the hope that someday they will suddenly develop empathy and a conscience for what they have been doing directly to their own grandchildren through the enabling and participation of psychological abuse to me as their mother.

There is generational dysfunction on both sides of the family in different ways. It was such an eye-opening experience to be on the inside of the dynamic within my in-law family unit for the years that I was. Although the underlying dysfunctional behaviours were very similar to my family of origin and the role I ended up playing in the end was identical in both families, on the outside at a surface level, they would appear to be completely different family units.

I saw high narcissistic traits from day one when meeting his family in the way of an extreme sense of entitlement, triangulation and subtly pitting family members against each other, lack of empathy, image management at all costs, extreme jealousy of others' successes, hiding the family secrets and dysfunction to the outside world and banding together to assist each other to avoid accountability, as well as the emotional climate of the family constantly revolving around toxic parents.

The first day I met his mother and the rest of the extended family, it was a family picnic at the beach. Everyone was on eggshells and the attention was on the mother, who was having an adult tantrum about things not being her way. Everyone was bending over backwards to appease the mother, to not rock the boat, to give her what she needed despite it being unreasonable.

My first interaction with her was as cold as ice. I felt prickly all over my body. I now know that feeling to be the vibe or energy someone gives off, and it was my nervous system and intuition responding adversely to her. Over the years, this pattern of my ex-partner and his siblings orbiting around the mother's moods, demands and tantrums became the normal. She was highly critical of everyone, extremely judgemental and outwardly jealous of others. Because of my fear of rejection and my experience with my family of origin and being scapegoated, I unconsciously shut out my authentic self and did everything I could to please and appease his mother to avoid rejection or judgement. I tried to be who I thought I needed to be so she would accept me. Looking back now, it was impossible for anything long lasting, as she found the negative in everything and everyone and was completely void of empathy or compassion.

On one occasion, I recall her bitterly criticising a good friend of hers who had tragically lost her husband only a year before. She was putting her down saying she's sick of hearing about her dead husband and it's been over a year now and that she needs to just get over it. I remember feeling shocked at hearing this about someone who was supposed to be a good friend of hers. It felt insensitive and just cruel. I realise now that this was a woman who had never experienced genuine love her entire life and lived her life through control and manipulation of her children and those around her. She simply could not relate to the genuine grief of losing someone you actually love. There was a void of any emotion. It simply couldn't be felt.

She was a caregiver void of emotional attunement, emotionally unavailable, and focused on image management to the detriment of the needs of her children. So, there was bound to be trauma, dysfunction, and unhealthy conditioning passed on to her children. My ex-partner, the "Golden Child", grew to be manipulative, devoid of empathy, has a superiority complex, is a pathological liar, and fosters a deep jealousy of others, while adopting a façade to always look good to the outside world. Integrity was virtually non-existent. Good was only done when people were watching or when he could receive recognition, and the darkest of things were done when no one was looking and well-hidden to the outside world.

There was another sibling who was the invisible child and who the family looked down on and pitied to make themselves feel more. She developed mental health issues in the way of deep depression and addiction issues and was admitted into a rehabilitation centre multiple times for substance abuse issues and suicidal ideation during the few years I was a part of the family. I had such a fondness for this sibling. She differed from the rest of them. She actually had a heart and compassion and I could see she was only troubled because of her low self-worth from the lifelong criticism and pressure to perform to which she wasn't able to live up to.

There was one particular occasion when another family member was having a christening for one of their children. The sibling who was in rehabilitation for alcohol and addiction issues arranged a half day pass out of the rebab centre to attend the christening event. During the morning tea after the service, the entire family sat around drinking beer and champagne in front of her at 11:00am in the morning. I was mortified. I was looking around and realising I was the only one in the room attuned to and noticing this sibling, who was sitting there in a deeply uncomfortable and somewhat distressed state. She was on day leave from a residential alcohol rehabilitation and the entire family was sitting around drinking in front of her with complete disregard to her reality and experience in life.

There was another disturbing revelation, where a family member shared with my ex-partner and I that they had experienced inappropriate sexual conduct from a priest at their mother's church when they were a young child. They expressed that on telling their mother when they were a teenager, the mother disregarded it, never spoke to them about it again and continued going to the same church. This invalidation and message that it's more important to maintain an image with a group, person or organisation that is superior, than to protect your child or stand up for your child, is one of the most damaging things a parent can do. This family member is completely unconscious and accepts the dysfunction in the family. It's as though they band together at all costs to keep the family dysfunction and secrets hidden from the outside world, while appearing to be functional, generous and good to the outsiders.

Their father had extensive affairs and years of cheating on his wife and to this day is not sorry for such actions and publicly says so. She stayed. I observed such deep hate between the parents for the entire time I was a part of their family. The dynamic was so obviously toxic that early in our relationship my ex-partner emailed his parents telling them that if they didn't change or fix their toxic and dysfunctional ways, fighting and putting him and his sibling in the middle of their issues, then when we had children, they would not be left alone with them as grandparents and they wouldn't be visiting them at their home. I still have a copy of this email communication. At the time my ex-partner wrote this to his parents, he was seeking an out and an alternative reality to escape to. Being with me and his belief at the time that he was going to adopt my family who seemed functional, with brothers-in-law for him to bond with and lots of laughter and fun times you could see from a surface glance, he turned his back on his own family and put himself above them on a pedestal and began talking down to them and their dysfunction. He acknowledged many times that he knew they were narcissistic, and we had many conversations about this over the years, both verbally and in emails.

Interestingly, once my family estrangement occurred during our wedding year, he automatically reverted to speaking highly of his family and pretending the dysfunction wasn't there and putting the projection onto me and my family as being less than. It was like he needed to fit somewhere and feel superior and was searching for that. To this day, he has turned a blind eye to his family's dysfunction, and they continue to enable his behaviour and do not hold him accountable. It's like giving him superpowers to feel invincible for the corruption and abuse as he gets away with it. His mother was well aware of the domestic violence that occurred during our relationship, and despite ringing me to beg me to give her son another chance when I tried to leave after the second physical assault, she completely gaslit me and denied everything after we separated to protect her family image. This allowed my ex-partner to avoid accountability once again and therefore never get the help he needed to make a genuine change. He was raised to lie, to cover up abuse and dysfunction, to blame others, and to never feel like he was in the wrong. He had developed an inflated sense of self and lived through his ego.

His father would state openly that he was not sorry for the affairs he continued to have for years, and often claimed my ex-partners mother deserved it because she was such a nagger. My ex-partner also agreed that he doesn't blame his dad for having an affair and cheating on his mother repeatedly because of the way his mother is. This caused extensive arguments between us, as I couldn't understand this belief or mindset that was making excuses for the occurrence of extramarital affairs. It was yet another red flag and like clockwork, my ex-partner had affairs to which he has never held himself accountable for and likely has the same belief that he is excused for these actions because of how I as his partner was.

Learnt behaviours, poor values that lack integrity, instilled a sense of entitlement to do as he pleased, despite the harm it causes others. A significant role model of my ex-partner was involved in unethical business affairs with overseas companies and I realise now only after our separation that this role model had been assisting and advising my ex-partner on how to hide his assets and finances from his marriage and to protect them in the event of divorce, all while coming after every penny I had within my superannuation, pre-marriage assets and our own children's savings accounts that were meant for their schooling. They were ruthless and disturbingly dishonest where finances were concerned during our separation.

They strategically planned to bypass and manipulate the court system and their tactic was to bully me so I would back down and not speak up or demand a fair settlement. Evidence of all this came to light during our separation but the depth of deceit and illegal lengths they will go to in order to cover up their conduct was extreme and most people wouldn't even come close to sleeping at night after having conducted themselves in such a way.

I believe karma has a way of working itself out. Unfortunately, my lived experience with these people has shown me that the people that raised him are not of integrity and shaped their son into a version of themselves where deceit, manipulation, greed, a lack of empathy and the absence of a conscience, was who he became at his core under the mask he wore. His parents, our children's grandparents, pushed him to drag me through family court for our property settlement, commit perjury, and contempt of court, all while they were in fact funding his legal fees to enable him to continue this insidious form of abuse aimed at creating maximum stress and impact on me in an attempt to force me to walk away. It was such a disgusting experience to witness from the grandparents of our children, with them knowing full well that their grandchildren were also on the receiving end of their treatment, with their quality of life and stability being severely impacted by what they were doing. I realise they are a different breed and do not possess values of integrity, compassion, or personal responsibility, and it is not within their capacity to feel or connect with the emotions or experience of others.

I recall on our wedding day his father did a speech. The speech included a few words about me as their daughter-in-law. I was so incredibly embarrassed, it was like he recited my resume and my career achievements and was completely void of emotion or anything that resembled any depth or any focus on who I actually am as a person. It was like bragging to the audience and big noting my achievements only. I was incredibly embarrassed and uncomfortable and wanted the floor to swallow me up. It was all a big show. No depth, no emotion, and nothing of meaning. That is what's important to them, looking good and image management. What you achieve and how you make them look is of the utmost importance. Not if you are happy, or who you are as a person. It just wasn't in their focus or of any importance to this family at all. Although I keep the door open for communication and connection to our children, they don't make any effort at this stage.

I know deep down this is for the best and the least influence they have on our young children the better. It is still extremely sad, however, and I still hold so much grief and guilt about the idea of what our children could and should have had in extended family. They deserve to have a sense of belonging, to receive unconditional love and to be surrounded by a village that can connect with them and always have their best interest at heart.

We all have aspects of generational trauma to varying degrees. The real measure is whether we continue to pass on unhealthy conditioning or whether we choose to pave a new way of love and connection, instead of a projection of generational pain.

CHAPTER 7

THE DOWNWARD SPIRAL

Our wedding day had passed, and although my family attended my wedding, they didn't speak to me on the day aside from my mother loudly and in-genuinely telling me she loved me when she could see she was in earshot of my mother-in-law watching to ensure she overheard. I was surrounded and suffocated by image management and inauthentic interactions from both families. Months passed after our wedding and I had not heard from my family since my wedding day, which reaffirmed that attending was all just about saving face.

I found out on my wedding morning that I was pregnant with our first child and I kept this to myself until sharing the news with my ex -partner at the end of our wedding night. He was pretty drunk but seemed over the moon about the news, which was a relief. There was a time around twelve weeks into the pregnancy, where I was working full-time while experiencing debilitating and relentless morning sickness. One evening during this time, my ex-partner had some unrest occur at his work with an impending organisational restructure along with his performance in his role being criticised, which placed him at risk of losing his job or getting demoted. He became consumed with this and instead of reflecting on the feedback he was being given about the issues with his work and what he needed to do better, he focused on his boss being the problem and reached out to others in his team to backstab his management and try to seek validation from his peers and get them on side. He became obsessed and consumed with this ongoing drama and trying to recruit his colleagues to his cause.

On the same evening, I began experiencing abdominal pain that progressed to unbearable levels. I was bedridden and debilitated and couldn't move or function at all. It was excruciating. I thought I must be having a miscarriage, or that something was wrong with the baby. I tried to call out to my then partner to where he was in the front office, and he eventually came in. He saw me in pain and became almost annoyed that I was taking his attention away from his current focus and my need for support was ever so inconvenient to him. He told me he had a few urgent things to attend to, advised me to get some rest and walked out. A short while later into the night, the pain became so bad that I felt I needed to call an ambulance or get to the hospital. I called out to him to ask for his help. He came in and when I asked if he could assist me in getting to a hospital, he shut me down saying he was waiting to hear from a colleague from work on an update on the restructure and he couldn't go anywhere at this stage. He left me in pain in the bedroom, unable to move.

He never checked on me for the rest of the night and after needing to down as many pain killers as I could find and safely take, to get some relief, I fell asleep in the early hours of the morning. I woke in the morning still in discomfort but much better and noticed he was getting ready to head off to work. He didn't even ask or check in on how I was. He went off to work like he was the only person who existed in the world, completely consumed by the dramas of his work situation. I got myself off to work that morning having my own commitments to fulfil. I felt exhausted and still in discomfort and feeling like I was the biggest burden in the world for needing support. This became a pattern in our relationship and my needs continued to be ignored, overridden, or invalidated.

On reflection of this pattern in my relationship, I realise now it was a core belief I carried originating from childhood that my needs are not important, that I am a burden if I speak up and ask for help and that I'm selfish if I voice my need for support that may affect another person's priorities. I was living out these beliefs into my adult life and re-creating the circumstances where I was attracting people who align with these limiting beliefs I held about myself. He did not see my needs as important. In fact, my needs were an inconvenience when as far as he was concerned, I was there to make him look good, support his dreams, provide him with a landing pad when things in his own world were unstable, and to bring me out to play when it suited him.

Narcissists cannot put another person's needs in front of their own unless they can gain recognition or gain some sort of benefit for themselves. They don't have the capacity to feel genuine empathy for others, so seeing someone upset or in pain has no impact on them and does not drive them to support others or change their behaviour unless there is a benefit or some sort of short or long-term gain or recognition in it for themselves. I would see this pattern play out repeatedly over the next few years of our relationship and would sadly see our children on the receiving end of the same treatment following our separation.

Another red flag was the various forms of coercive control around finances. I had worked very hard and established my assets and financial security prior to meeting him and owned multiple properties. I had established investments that were structured to be paid off and become my superannuation for retirement. I was secure and felt in a good position to start a family and take a step back from full-time work when I had children.

Just before I was due to have our first child, my ex-partner was pressuring me to put one of my home loans on hold and change the structure so I had more money coming into our spending account that would result in my home loan not being paid off while I was on paid maternity leave. It did not seem to be a smart financial decision, and we didn't need the extra money for spending as we were both bringing in an income through my maternity leave period. He pressured me so much and, when I wouldn't agree, he contacted my bank without my knowing, of which he was not even a member of and tried to directly request himself that they change my home loan. As the home and loan were in my name only, the bank insisted I give consent. Without even knowing that he had contacted the bank, he approached me one afternoon and quickly said the bank was on the phone and I needed to give them consent that he has permission to talk to them about my loan on my behalf. He held the phone to my ear and put me on the spot without allowing me time to even think. I answered a couple of questions and said yes to him being able to speak with them. He then went out of the house, so I was out of earshot and changed everything on my loan to exactly what I'd told him I didn't want to do. It all happened so quickly and when confronting him, it turned to an argument, so I ended up letting it go to keep the peace and avoid stress during my final stage of pregnancy.

Not long before this time, he had casually told me he had some funds in an overseas account that he wanted to bring to Australia for our future. I didn't know the details and when he said he needed to get my bank account details so he could transfer it to my account to put against another investment home loan I had, it seemed to make sense and I didn't think too much of it. Little did I know he was attempting to use me as a pawn for him to commit tax evasion, so it would not be detected as coming to his account from overseas. I had no idea about any of this sort of stuff and was so naïve and complacent.

During our separation it was to become prevalent that he had finances hidden overseas our entire relationship and he, with the support from his parents, played the tax system and eventually the Family Court System during our separation and could move these funds further offshore to ensure they were un-traceable within the family court system processes.

Another similar circumstance was that I discovered that he had committed fraud and used my identification documents without my consent to sign me up to a betting and gambling account in my name, but for his use and access only. When I discovered this, I challenged it and requested it be closed down. I am not a gambler. Gambling does not align with my values, and I was uncomfortable knowing that it was even possible for someone to pretend to be me and establish a gambling account with my identity. It progressed to an argument, and he refused to close it down as it had become a syndicate for a group of his friend's interstate. I remained discontent with this account and it caused much tension over the next couple of years.

One day when I was at work, he called me and said they had locked the betting account because of suspected identification fraud, and he said I had to call up and pretend it was mine to have it unlocked. I was so angry. It put me into a position where he expected me to lie and commit a crime to cover for him and have his account unlocked. I refused to do it. He pressured me and fought with me for days until the stress was so much that I said I would call them up to unlock it just to get him off my case. I called them and the consultant drilled me telling me that if I had shared my account with someone, I could be fined and charged. I was devastated. I felt so angry at my ex-partner for putting me in such a position. I gave him an ultimatum that he had to close the account or I would report him to the betting company for my identity fraud. I had had enough of the control and being taken advantage of. Somehow through all of this, he turned this situation to be about me being too uptight. It was crazy making how he had this ability to always flip and project the situation to be about me being the problem.

Later on, during the early period in our separation, I found out I had an extra home loan in my name that I didn't know about. We had fought to no end about a maximum loan amount I was willing to be a part of for a new home he insisted we build. He tried to convince me to have a high amount, but the risk was too great, and I refused. Little did I know, that on the evening before I was due to deliver our second child by caesarean section because of a last-minute complication, he placed bank documents under my nose and casually told me to initial the front page and explained it was just the loan we had discussed. I signed without even thinking twice about it. After all, it had been very clear what I had agreed to in all our heated discussions previously. After we separated, it came to light there were two loans and one of them I did not even know about and it was in a bank profile I didn't know existed, yet it was a joint loan in both our names. He had been paying it off from our joint savings. I realised that night before our baby was born, he had waited until I was distracted and complacent to manipulate and trick me into signing bank documents, all while giving me the impression it was the loan amount we discussed. He had strategically disguised this behaviour of manipulating to get what he wanted at all costs throughout our entire relationship.

The nights out drinking, frequent all-nighters to strip clubs, weeks away on leisure sailing trips and race events still continued. It continued to cause tension and issues in our relationship. Nothing had changed. I was isolated from my family and very vulnerable. As a result, his sense of entitlement became more inflated and his already low concern for consequences of his actions became more prevalent. It was like he believed I was in a position where I could never leave him now. That is how I actually felt deep down. I felt trapped, like I had no choice but to bear it, accept it, and make it work.

Now that he was in my home and in control of all my assets. Now that he had successfully groomed my best friends into believing he was an amazing and generous partner and planted the seeds that me and my family of origin were the issues of our past marital tension all along. It was the perfect scenario for him. The pretty little wife, who could add to his financial portfolio, who was too insecure to speak up to the dysfunction and now had nowhere to go and no one to confide in. It was the perfect scenario for him to continue having his needs met and doing as he pleases in life, while still maintaining the image of a happy family life and give the impression to outsiders of having it all.

THE DEPTH OF HER SURVIVAL

He focused on trying to climb the status ladder in his work. He was obsessed with fitting in with the popular crowd at work and used this as the excuse to always head out on weekends or for after-work drinks instead of coming home to help with our child or the evening routine. I was in such a traumatised and shut down state from what had occurred in our wedding year and the extreme betrayal from my mother and ostracisation from my family that I couldn't feel anything. I was frozen. Dissociated. Just unconsciously functioning in life. Putting one foot in front of the other every day to keep going. Putting a smile on my face when I needed to, performing to the highest of levels at work and pretending everything was fine.

There was also a time way back during our first pregnancy, and another blatant red flag moment that, in hindsight, was a clear sign of what was to come. We ended up in an argument about his drinking habits again. I didn't let up this time as I remember thinking this behaviour had to stop before the baby arrived. I needed to make it stop. The discussion became heated and I recall feeling very triggered by the repeat projection and back tracking on previous promises that change would be made. Actions never matching words, and broken promises, over and over again. In short, he became enraged and punched a hole right through the wall in the hallway of the home we lived in and the home I owned. That hole remained there for the next few years and he covered it with a mirror and acted like nothing had happened. I told my then best friend about this event the day it occurred and the following day, once we had resolved our argument, we were invited over to this friend's place to have a BBQ with her and her husband. The disturbing thing was that on arrival, her husband and his brother, who were also there, began hi-fiving my ex-partner and calling him Jacky Chan, after the Asian karate fighter movie hero. This violent and volatile behaviour was a joke and something to be praised for being macho. He was given so much attention that he was clearly enjoying it, and it changed his attitude from being remorseful to that of acting as if what he had done wasn't even that bad. I remember feeling so invalidated and questioned if maybe I was over-reacting in thinking this type of behaviour wasn't acceptable.

Not too long into our separation period, this same enabling of my ex-partner continued from this friend, and I am no longer friends with these people as there is no place in my life for toxic connections. I can see how toxic this friendship was all along in enabling my abuser and invalidating my evidenced experience. Not once was I asked if I was okay or given any sort of acknowledgement that this attempt to scare and intimidate me by punching a hole in the wall of our home was not acceptable. It wasn't until I had to sell that home during our divorce that the hole was repaired, and he admitted through legal proceedings and was called out because he had, in fact, damaged the property in a fit of rage.

The night before our first baby was due to be born by induction, we had been invited to a wedding. I wanted to go, and it was someone important to me, but I was cautious and feeling anxious as it was in another town and I expected a difficult labour and birth the next day. Not to mention the thought of standing for hours in high heels well into the night was not appealing at nine months pregnant. My ex-partner really wanted to go and so we attended. I had a serious talk with him about my concerns and we established he would not drink and would drive us to our hotel accommodation close by to the wedding. It was a two-hour drive to the hospital we booked in for the birth so it was a risk to be staying away so close to our due date, but we agreed that if he wouldn't drink, then at least he could drive us to the hospital in the night if needed.

It was a lovely wedding, and I was happy to be there. As we moved into the evening, I noticed my ex-partner was drinking, despite our agreement, and he became quite tipsy. He was never without a drink in his hand. It really hit me hard to see him completely disregarding our arrangement, but to avoid confrontation, I said nothing. It was like he had just told me what I wanted to hear to get me to agree to go to the wedding, but had no intentions of following through on his word. All the promises and commitments out the window, with complete disregard for how I would have been feeling only twenty four hours prior to giving birth to our first child.

As the night went on, he became completely blind drunk. He was having a good old time. When it reached 11pm at night, I asked him if we could head back to our accommodation. I was exhausted. I was feeling anxious about the birth. He disregarded my request and said he wasn't ready to go yet and took off for more socialising. I waited patiently for another hour and on almost midnight and, feeling myself go into a bit of a panic and overwhelm, I firmly told him we were leaving. It still took another while for him to actually leave and by this stage, he was slurring his words and couldn't string a sentence together.

We eventually got to the car and the minute he sat in the passenger seat, he passed out. I drove to our accommodation in tears. Feeling so exhausted, unsupported and betrayed. I was reflecting on our deep conversations about attending the wedding and the agreement we put in place to ensure it was safe and suitable for us to attend with our impending birth. In the morning, I said nothing. We headed back to our hometown and got ourselves ready to head to the hospital. I could feel my nervous system was activated. I was scared. I knew I couldn't rely on him to support me through this. I was overwhelmed by having a baby without a supportive mother in my life. Things felt so big and heavy, and I felt so alone. At some level, I knew that what I had gotten myself into with this man was a big mistake, but it was too late now. I had to block it out and make it work. I didn't have a family now and had to ensure I made it work with him. After all, we had a baby on its way in only a few hours' time.

The birth was traumatic. It was a failed induction that required medical intervention and resulted in our little baby needing emergency resuscitation for quite some time and being placed in intensive care for a few days. During the early phase of the labour when things got really painful and hard, I suddenly had a complete panic attack and melt down about my mother and why she did what she did, why she didn't care and why she wasn't able to be a loving and supportive mother. On reflection, it was immense suppressed grief being released through my body. My ex-partner messaged my mother and asked her to contact me, explaining I was in labour. Although I didn't know at the time that he had asked her to message me, this is one thing I appreciated about him during this experience as receiving the message from her, although likely not a genuine message, gave me a sense of comfort in that moment that she cared, and I could let go and move forward in my labour.

I remember after a twenty-five hour labour, our baby being whisked away before I even held or saw him. There was no crying and no movement. He was discoloured, and I knew something wasn't right. I lay there in the birth suite alone, still covered in blood, while my ex-partner and the medical team went with our baby. What I remember in that moment of seeing them resuscitating our baby, seeing the lack of vital signs on the machines and observing the expressions of concern and urgency from the medical team, it crossed my mind that he might not survive. I also noticed that I felt almost nothing. I put it down to exhaustion, but I recognise I had almost no response to what was unfolding in front of my eyes. It was like an out-of-body experience where I was observing it, but I had no emotional connection to it. What I now understand this to be is a coping mechanism of dissociation. I was already numb and somewhat disconnected in this phase in life after the trauma from my family's ostracisation and resulting estrangement, and with the ongoing betrayals and lack of support from my ex-partner that left me feeling unsafe in my relationship and inner world. Having such a traumatic labour and then the realisation that my baby might not survive, my system shut down any emotional feeling at all. I didn't panic, I didn't cry, I didn't speak. I just did nothing. And waited. After a long while, a nurse came in to check on me. She stopped to look at me and commented on how calm I appeared to be considering the circumstances. She praised me for being so brave. I smiled politely and continued to wait, numb, feeling nothing.

Moving forward and having our baby with us at home, life went back to normal. I was on maternity leave, and he got back to the intensity of his work and his weekend hobbies. He soon became bored with the mundane life of a newborn baby routine and although he helped when he was at home, he went back to the after work drinks, the sporting events on weekends and the nights out. Because of the birth I had, I needed a longer recovery than what would typically be expected for a natural birth. I was also still in traumatic shock at not having a supportive mother or family for this phase of my life. I needed, more than anything, a supportive husband for these early times of our first new born baby. The lack of support I experienced as a new mother and in this relationship was a pattern and program I had playing out my entire life. Before having my own children, I coped with this by adopting hyper-independence and not relying on anyone, simply because I had no one in my life that had truly been supportive and had my back. Once my children came along, support is something I needed most. The hyper-independence didn't fit or work in this phase of life or circumstances. I realised now that my lack of self-worth and a belief that I wasn't worthy of support allowed for and drew into my world, more of the same. Lack of support. I was craving it and begging for support in my relationship, and it gave my personal power away to my toxic ex-partner as it made him feel as though I needed him and he therefore didn't need to make an effort or even consider my needs.

It reinforced my core belief that I was a burden for asking for help or having needs in this relationship. It wasn't until much later in my separation that I really unravelled this belief and reprogrammed it to my new alignment of increased self-worth. It would be a long and treacherous road to get to this time. I had such a long way to go on my personal healing journey from this current point.

CHAPTER 8

THE POINT OF NO RETURN

One morning, when our baby was ten weeks old, I was breastfeeding him on the bed for his early morning feed. My ex-partner was getting ready for work and casually told me he had booked himself to go away for a few weeks on a sailing event up north that was upcoming in a location fifteen hours away. He was obsessed with sailing. All his weekends were committed to sailing. We had little to no time together, which caused a growing disconnection that I couldn't seem to rectify. I naturally had reservations about him leaving for weeks when we had a newborn at home and no support around. On expressing my feeling of upset about his insistence that he was going, I started crying and felt the usual weight and heaviness of the chronic lack of support. He became rather irritated that I was expressing emotion and voicing my needs in this situation. The more aggressive and colder he became in his communication to me, the more triggered and upset I became about not being heard and not feeling I had any support.

What happened next and the impact it had on me, was to be the end of any chance for our relationship to work, but I wouldn't realise this until years later. He began yelling at me and putting me down to silence me. I felt my whole body tremble involuntarily, and I began hyperventilating and couldn't breathe. It filled me with panic. Our baby was still attached to my breast feeding but had fallen asleep in that position. I was kneeling on the bed, cradling the baby in the feeding position. Panic overcame me and I put the baby on the bed in front of me as I attempted to run out of the room. Just before I reached the doorway, he launched at me. He grabbed me around my throat, strangling me with one of his hands, and thrust me up and into the wall by my neck. I was hanging in the air by my throat, completely choking in his grasp. I couldn't move. I couldn't breathe. I couldn't scream.

I remember the terror I felt, and how I attempted to scream, but no words came out. There was no breath. I was suffocating for what felt like ages. I began trying to kick my legs, and he finally dropped me to the ground. I immediately tried to scream at him in terror, but no words came out. It was just a rasp. I had instantly lost my voice. I couldn't swallow because of the pain in my neck and throat. With every attempt to swallow my oesophagus would click and move sideways.

I went back and grabbed our baby from the bed, and I ran. I ran to the garage and into the car and locked the door. My entire body was trembling. I was in a complete state of shock. My neck and throat were throbbing with pain. I couldn't swallow and my head wasn't able to turn fully sideways and was locked up. I was terrified. The baby was crying. I was crying. He was in my home. That used to be my safe space. I couldn't think. I didn't have anywhere to go. So, I just drove. I drove like a deer in the headlights. I ended up in a town in the hinterland region an hour away. I found an Airbnb, and I stayed there in the room for a few nights with the baby. It was the middle of winter and was freezing. The lady who let us into the room knew something was up. She came back with firewood and gave me her number in case I needed anything.

I lay in bed, feeding our baby in a frozen and shocked state for two days straight. The biggest mistake I made was not reaching out to someone and telling someone. I didn't feel like I could tell anyone. I hadn't even considered telling the authorities, as he was the father of my child. I stayed silent. I had a ten week old baby and was still recovering from the birth. I didn't have a support network outside of friends who all thought he was amazing, and I didn't think I could do it on my own. I continued to receive text messages from him, trying to intimidate me into taking the blame and accept it was all my fault. It was awful. When I insisted he had to move out and that our relationship was over, he progressively began shifting the other way and acting as if he was completely remorseful and full of apologies while begging me to come home.

I eventually grabbed at the fantasy that he was sorry and that it wouldn't happen again, so I could go home and not have to do this on my own. I couldn't actually leave and I think deep down I knew this. I allowed myself to go back and believed he was sorry and that it wouldn't happen again. Little did I know that this remorse was far from genuine and it would come to light during our separation period later just how little remorse he had for this hideous assault that occurred in the presence of our new born baby.

The calculating behaviour to cover up this act and to twist the narrative to avoid accountability would present early in our separation and cause immense re-traumatisation. Despite this volatile assault, I did not yet know the depth of who and what I was dealing with until the mask fell off and stayed off for good during our separation.

I had sunk into a deep depression after this assault, but no one would have noticed. I could pretend to people in the outside world, that things were fine. I secretly sought counselling with a psychologist for the first time in my life and on my first appointment where I was feeling like I didn't know if I could go on for much longer in this state, I was told that I had adjustment disorder from my family situation. I didn't resonate with this at all. I also didn't even tell her about my marital issues or the recent assault at all, so there was no way she was going to help me.

I was screaming on the inside for her to just know what I was feeling and the depth of despair I was in. I couldn't voice it. I never shared the truth with this psychologist about what he had recently done with the physical abuse. I was beating around the bush and not being clear about what was really going on. I sat there calmly breastfeeding my baby, appearing to have it together. I left the appointment feeling like she had no idea how much I was truly struggling. I went a few more times and then found it was pointless and was just creating more stress trying to get to an appointment with a newborn baby in tow, so I stopped going. I was like a walking zombie. I joined a mother's group but went infrequently in the early days. I was so unsupported at home in these initial months post birth and there was regular abuse in various forms escalating from my ex-partner now that I was in such a vulnerable state, that I couldn't find the motivation or energy to go out and socialise regularly.

The Point of No Return

I got to where I decided I needed to snap out of it and make some changes, so I coped by trying to create experiences to show myself and the world that I was okay and happy. I began arranging social events and activities for my ex-partner to always be stimulated. He was happy when busy. He seemed to be more content and treated me better. It was a distorted version of the saying "happy wife, happy life", when in fact my belief and what I was trying to execute was a happy husband, safe wife.

I was disconnected but appeared to be highly functioning. I went back to fulltime work when our baby was seven months old and got stuck back into the hustle of life for distraction. My physical health began taking a hit. Being someone who had always been so health conscious, fit and strong, it was an unexpected downward slide of my health. I had these unexplainable and involuntary twitches in bed every night, where my whole body would spasm and twitch. It only occurred at night while lying next to him in bed. It lasted for a couple of years. I know this now to be my nervous system, completely dysregulated and a trauma response from being in proximity to my ex-partner. I also shut down from intimacy. I couldn't let him touch me and I would freeze up. We were literally only intimate on maybe two occasions to conceive a second child, which was another attempt at distraction in having another child to focus on and to keep moving forward in life.

There were many other symptoms that manifested from the trauma I was experiencing and the resulting inflammation in my body. I developed unexplained body rashes and skin lesions that wouldn't go away, and when seeking medical tests, nothing would show. This skin disorder stayed for over three years and miraculously healed up for good within six months of leaving my ex-partner. I also had severe abdominal episodes of pain that were so bad that I needed to be hospitalised on morphine, and this pain also could not be diagnosed. I had numerous tests, but nothing showed up. These episodes became excessively worse towards the end of our marriage and increased during the stress of the early separation. There were also chronic thyroid issues and abnormal kidney levels that began during this relationship that were unexplained by the medical professionals. After having these painful episodes occur every few months for years during the relationship, I haven't had one in the years since leaving.

People who experience narcissistic abuse and other forms of domestic violence, on top of developing mental health symptoms from the trauma, are often diagnosed with chronic pain, autoimmune disorders and chronic illness and eventually chronic fatigue, because of long-term exposure to cortisol and adrenaline which are the fight-or-flight chemicals. These stress hormones cause immense inflammation in the body. Inflammation causes pain, or worse, it causes your immune system to attack itself because it thinks the inflammation is caused by a disease it needs to eradicate.

This adds another complex layer of risk to the health and potential life of those who stay in such relationships. It's not only the physical risk of a volatile and unpredictable partner eventually having an episode that results in extreme harm or worse, but it's the very real risk to your health and life through chronic and toxic stress that there is no reprieve from. Through my experience, I have been drawn to study the link between trauma and chronic illness and the manifestation of symptoms and conditions from stress and unresolved trauma. There is an undeniable link that I have discovered through not only research but through having experienced it first-hand. I now support many clients experiencing chronic health issues linked to their unresolved trauma in the work I do in the holistic mental health space.

CHAPTER 9

LOOK WHAT YOU MADE ME DO

There became a carelessness and obvious complacency within my ex-partner, in that he knew exactly how to manipulate me and the relationship. I was still so caught up in hope and listening to the words spoken and the future promises made. Instead, I needed to be strong and conscious to look at the obvious repeat actions that never seemed to match his words, no matter how many arguments, upset or near loss of our relationship it caused. I honestly believe he thought now I didn't have my family support, that now we had children and that he had seen, I would continue to forgive time and time again no matter what he did; he thought I would never leave him. There was a time where I felt completely trapped and that this was actually the case. He created circumstances where he would knowingly re-offend and do whatever he pleased, and blatantly disregard my attempts to set boundaries. He knew all he had to do was to deal with the consequences of my upset later on, proceed with his manipulation and tell me the words I wanted to hear, and I'd eventually forgive and stay. The damage this pattern did to my self-worth and confidence was detrimental. I allowed someone to continue to destroy me with repeat behaviours and could not find the capacity or self-respect to leave. It was soul destroying.

By the time our first child was a year old, I was well on the path to becoming aware of what I was stuck in. Or so I thought. I realise now that I did not know the depth or reality of what I was dealing with or what resided under the mask of the person I had married. I still didn't think I could or would actually leave him with the cognitive dissonance I had playing out that was continuing to create such mental confusion and confliction in what I thought and believed to be true with him. I didn't have clarity on whether he really was this evil and abusive narcissistic partner who was intentionally choosing these behaviours, or if he was in fact the partner who was just struggling to navigate his childhood conditioning and he could change to the person, he promised he would be moving forward. I also took on his projection that there was something wrong with me and I was unlovable. There was even a period, in my desperation to find a solution for the abuse, where I was convinced that he had Asperger's and was on the spectrum. He also tried to convince me this was the case, instead of having me see the truth of his repeat behaviours being something intentional and sinister. He even agreed to attend complementary therapy I arranged for him in desperation to address the brain functioning issues that are present in those on the spectrum.

I was desperate to fix whatever was causing these ongoing toxic and harmful behaviours in our relationship. Around this time, he discussed extensively with me how his father displayed antisocial personality traits, lack of empathy, a sense of entitlement and no remorse, and he acknowledged that he thought his issues were due to how he was raised. He acknowledged his mother had high narcissistic traits and that her lack of empathy, high criticism and extreme need for control had detrimentally impacted him and his siblings. He had me believing that he understood and he got it and that he wanted to change to move his behaviours away from following in the footsteps of the generational dysfunction he had been repeating.

There was one of his siblings in particular, that he actually asked me to contact to offer her support for her mental health challenges. He had acknowledged that he knew her symptoms resulted from low self-worth from her upbringing, and in particular, his highly critical and controlling mother. All of this was acknowledged and in fact led by him, and I realise now that although he does very much have the awareness of these things being the case, he doesn't actually care or want to change it. It's almost like his need to avoid accountability and therefore never have to deal with his deep shame, results in him trying to deny and hide his family dysfunction as they provide him with the admiration he craves and they enable him to keep being the way he is without having to change or to ever be accountable for his behaviour. My observation is that it works both ways in that his parents also benefit by enabling him, as he will also cover and hide their dysfunction from the outside world in return.

When our first child had just gone twelve months old, my ex-partner pushed and coerced me into complying and agreeing to renovate and sell an investment property I'd had for ten years and long before I met him and had set it up to be my superannuation for retirement. I didn't want to sell and the force and dominance in which he took over this property to sell and acquire the funds from was extreme. It caused so much tension and arguments that wore me down. Once he got what he wanted and was successful in taking over and selling it, he tried to apologise and manipulate me in to thinking he had reflected and was sorry for forcing me in to something I was so strongly against. It didn't change the outcome. He had what he wanted. This really shook me up, and I felt so disempowered, as if nothing I said or did would ever have him respect or listen to my needs, wants, or desires. Following this situation, there was an obvious disconnection between us. I was so shut down to him.

He continued going out drinking to all hours of the night, leaving me home with the baby and trying to manage full-time work and doing the bulk of the caring for our child after hours. The resentment and exhaustion began building within me. One night when he was out late drinking, I was home with our baby who was unwell with a vomiting bug. He was vomiting repeatedly through the night to where the only way I could manage it was to have him lie on the shower floor with the water running over him while he slept and vomited periodically through the night. I lay on the bathroom tiles with him until the early hours of the morning. It was a stressful and exhausting night.

My ex-partner came home after midnight and walked into the bathroom blind drunk, wreaking of alcohol and just being disgusting. I was repulsed and agitated. I didn't want to wake our child, who was trying to sleep on the tiles in the shower, so I quietly hissed at him to get out of the bathroom. He immediately got his back up and bellowed at me that it was his house too now and his son too and he had every right to be in the bathroom. I reminded him we had another bathroom he could access to which he childishly stated he wanted to stay in this one. I felt the agitation rise within me but had to suppress it as I was trying to keep calm for our child. I told my ex-partner again to get out and reiterated that I'd been up all night with our unwell son while he had been out boozing it up, and I didn't want our son woken up by his drunken antics. I desperately needed space from him in this moment, as I was feeling so triggered and repulsed by his presence and his obvious sense of entitlement in this situation. He completely disregarded that our child was ill, and at the top of his voice began ranting and refused to leave the room. He progressed to yelling at me through slurred words.

By this stage, I was irate. I recall telling him he was a pig and continued to insist he leave the room. It was like his ego was so big and he was too arrogant and entitled to see the situation for what it was. Instead of doing what was right for his child, he had to stay and fight to win and have power over me. This situation ended in him snarling at me to *do everyone a favour and go and kill myself,* as I lay there with our child on the bathroom floor. It was revolting.

Despite my internal state and activation, I just stayed laying on the floor in silence, and he eventually got bored and walked out. As I lay there for the rest of the night, I knew I had to get out and leave this relationship. I had been through this so many times and I knew I had to escape.

The next day, I attempted to have a conversation to finish our relationship. It ended with him blaming me, putting me down, denying what had occurred, and twisting everything to say I was being unreasonable about his drinking habits. He labelled me a "teetotaller" which apparently means a prude who doesn't drink alcohol. His focus was on justifying that he doesn't drink more than anyone else's husbands and that I was the one with the problem and was being unreasonable. When he realised that his attacking approach was pushing me further away, like clockwork, he slowly reverted to the other extreme and it ended in remorse, apologies, future promises, attentiveness and him declaring his commitment that he was going to quit drinking all together for good. He claimed that if his behaviour whilst drinking was ruining his family, then he will quit drinking for good. This was a huge promise, and I challenged him on it repeatedly as I didn't believe him, but he insisted he meant it and gave his word. For whatever reason I allowed myself to believe this or think it was genuine is beyond me, but I did, and it had me holding onto hope that it was a step in the right direction for genuine change.

Within three days of this event, and him being ever so attentive and loving towards me, which allowed me to finally relax and have hope he was genuine this time, he took me and our son out for breakfast before work on this day. While we were there, he smoothly and manipulatively stated that he had a work function on that night that he claimed was mandatory for him to attend. I found this hard to believe, but he insisted he needed to go, and almost humbled himself to ask my permission, which made me feel bad if I was to say no or that I didn't approve.

Deep down I felt hurt that only days before, on a weeknight that we'd had such a horrendous experience with him after going out to a function on a weeknight, and now only days later and after promising he was quitting drinking for good, he was going out again to an alcohol fuelled event. It just felt a little too soon and, like the severity of what had just occurred, was forgotten. I quietly agreed that it's fine for him to go and he insisted he wouldn't drink and would be home at a reasonable time. This would prove to be more of the same pattern of manipulating me to get what he wanted and actions, not matching his words.

That evening, he headed out to the function straight from work. I got home from my day at work after having collected our baby from childcare and began the evening routine of getting him to bed. He was still having a bottle feed late at night at this stage. I stayed up to do his 11:30pm feed, and shortly after, just after midnight, my ex-partner walked through the door. I could tell instantly he had been drinking. I was tired and didn't have it in me to address this, so I simply raised my eyebrows at him and turned to walk down the hallway to go to the bedroom to get some sleep. As I turned to walk away, he snarled at me in an aggressive and extremely loud manner, stating, *"what's wrong with you now"*.

It instantly triggered me, considering he had promised to be home early and to not drink, which clearly wasn't the case. I turned around and faced him and told him to be quiet as our baby had just gone back to sleep and called him out on being drunk again. What happened next was frightening and instantly shut me down in fear. He completely lost his cool and began yelling at me and putting me down in an ongoing drunken rant, deflecting from what the issue at present actually was and almost trying to intimidate me with his behaviour. It woke our baby up who began crying from the nursery. He immediately progressed towards the nursery, so I stood myself in the doorway and told him he was not going into our baby's room in his drunken state. I told him to go away and that I'd tend to our baby. He became enraged. He tried to push his way past me to enter the nursery and I held firm in the doorway, telling him again he was drunk and that he was not going near our baby in that state. He then grabbed my arms and pulled me roughly out of the doorway. I tried to move myself back in between him and the doorway to prevent him from entering the nursery. What happened next was to change me forever and become something I would carry with me for the rest of my life. As I attempted to move myself back into the doorway to protect our baby from him entering, he thrust his fist into the air and punched me in the face at full force. I was instantly airborne and knocked to the ground about a metre or so away. My head cracked onto the tiled floor heavily as I landed. I don't remember some of what happened immediately after as I lost consciousness for a short time and what I recall next is waking up on the floor, with a pool of blood next to my face and my lip and jaw throbbing in pain. As I lay faced down, my entire body was trembling. I was frozen and couldn't move. My heart was pounding out of my chest. I just lay there, frozen, unable to move. I could hear him in our baby's nursery and our baby still crying as my ex-partner was yelling out to me on repeat in a panicked state, *"why did you make me do that!"*.

The sound of our baby crying eventually snapped me out of my immobilised state and I stood up, full of adrenaline and cortisol in a complete survival state of fight, and charged into the nursery, ripped the baby out of his hands and ran to the bedroom and locked the door. Fortunately, I settled our baby quickly back to sleep in my bed. He didn't try to come into the bedroom at all, to my relief.

A brief while later, I heard him begin talking to someone at the other end of the house. I timidly unlocked the door, crept out of the room, and stood in the hallway to listen. It was obvious it was his mother who he was speaking with. I heard him say in a panic, *"But I hit her, I hit her"*. The conversation lasted a while, and I eventually just went back to the bedroom and locked the door and stayed in there for the night. I stayed locked in the bedroom with our baby until I heard him leave the house the next morning.

The interesting thing I realise now is that it didn't even cross my mind to call the police after the assault occurred. It did not, in fact, cross my mind that what had occurred on this occasion and months earlier with the previous event of strangulation was, in fact, domestic violence.

Although I ended up telling my ex-partner I had gone to the hospital and it was recorded on my medical records and also that I reported it to the police to have it on record, this was to deter him from doing it again, but I didn't even consider reporting it to any sort of professional. It wasn't at all in my awareness that I should of or could have done so. This was to be one of my biggest mistakes and something that could have prevented the extent of abuse that occurred from him through the legal system during our separation, as he continually attempted to twist the narrative and flip roles painting me as the perpetrator and he as the victim. When he discovered I did not officially report it to a professional in those years prior, his legal representation advised him it was safe to lie and commit perjury in court as there was no admissible evidence in the criminal context despite there being photos, his direct admission of the assaults in text messages, psychologist notes, and a third party witness who had been informed in writing at the time the event occurred. Without a formal medical or police report, the way the legal system works provides a myriad of loopholes for those who can afford skilled and aggressive legal representation.

I contacted him by text that morning once he left the house and demanded he move out. The usual onslaught resulted in him trying to twist and distort the facts and avoiding accountability occurred as expected. I was adamant that he had to move out. I gave him the ultimatum that he had to move out, otherwise I would move out, renting elsewhere, and taking the baby with me. He finally agreed to move out temporarily, and he took our caravan and booked into a caravan park.

Once he had moved out, the apologies, begging for forgiveness and what was portrayed as remorse came in hard and fast from him in the following weeks. His mother called me multiple times, initially acknowledging the assault and sharing her own experience with my ex-partner's father about a physical altercation they had had. She very much blamed my ex-partner's father for her son's behaviour in our instance. Within a week, however, her tone and attitude towards me changed. She told me quite matter-of-factly that her son had been punished enough, and it was about time I allowed him to come home.

When I still insisted our relationship was over, she appeared very sad and bombarded me with guilt trips about how I would ruin the family and her grandchildren's lives if I didn't stop this nonsense about leaving her son.

I understand now that she had been in a similar situation to me, and she stayed. She stayed when her husband had multiple affairs and isn't sorry to this day. She stayed when she was physically assaulted. She stayed in a completely toxic and loveless marriage, and now she was expecting me to do the same. That's just what you do in her world and I would be ridiculed and shamed if I did not choose the same path and turn a blind eye to what was occurring in our relationship and accept it.

A few days after the incident, I received a message from my then best friend. She was asking me to join her in taking the babies out for a walk together as she also had a child the same age. I ended up disclosing over the message what had occurred a few days prior and explained I wasn't up for an outing just yet, as my face was still quite swollen and sore.

During my explanation, shame overtook me, and I felt so insecure sharing this information with anyone and I downplayed it. I ended up somewhat making excuses for him, but she still acknowledged at the time that it was something severe and unacceptable. This friend, would later in years to come, be completely manipulated by my ex-partner and during our separation she became someone who caused more harm and distress to me than good, in disregarding and invalidating my experience, turning her back on me, and enabling and supporting my ex-partner in his post separation abuse tactics.

Having someone you thought was a best friend betray you, put you in harm's way by enabling your abuser and turn on you during a crisis, was another level of trauma that I have since needed to heal and work through. A part of my healing journey was finally having boundaries with anyone who enables my ex-partner and invalidates my evidenced experience. I have let this friend and others connected to her go in recent years to avoid the ongoing re-traumatisation of being invalidated and judged and to remove the risk of my personal information being passed on through gossip. As difficult as this was to make this choice, it was vital for my healing. In fact, it was vital to my survival during the post-separation period for many reasons.

I reflected on the values that are important to me; friendships which are loyal, mutually supportive, compassionate, of integrity, and of kindness. Any friendship that does not represent these values in our connection is no longer in my inner world and is no longer what I would consider a genuine friendship. Holding onto people because they are familiar and out of fear of being alone or unsupported, is no longer a place I operate from. As we heal and elevate from the old version of ourselves, those that do not align, respect or honour this new version fall away.

After a few weeks of my ex-partner having moved out, I eventually succumbed to the continual manipulation, hoovering and love bombing, and eventually took a leap of faith and let him move back in. Once back home, it was like he was completely fine and acted as if nothing had even happened. I found it quite confronting, as I was still somewhat in a state of shock at what had occurred. Life went on as if nothing had happened and we never spoke of the recent event. He agreed to have couple's counselling but made me promise I wouldn't share our deeper personal issues during our sessions.

My involuntary body twitches and shut-down emotional state continued however, and I could barely let him touch me without freezing up. After about four weeks of this, I made the decision that I needed to make myself try to move on and let him back in emotionally. I would find out a few weeks later that I had fallen pregnant with our second child. It was a distraction and something to focus on. I was living in a constant state of fight and flight and on autopilot, just existing while appearing high functioning. I continued my work full time as I grew our baby, so I was very busy and, although exhausted, it stopped me from having time or space to actually think too much, which is what I needed at the time to cope.

Our second baby was born early the following year. In the lead up to the birth, I became quite overwhelmed at the thought of being so vulnerable again within the home once the baby came along. I would be on maternity leave, my body would need to repair and heal if the previous birth was anything to go by, and

I still had vivid memories of an unforgettable lack of support and horrendous physical violence I experienced in the early phase after our first baby was born.

I felt that to cope with this overwhelm, I needed to come up with a plan so I could feel safe and know I'd have the support and safety I needed. I ended up coming up with an idea to have a live-in au pair join our family for a couple of months in the newborn phase. We had the space, and I was on paid maternity leave so we could afford this, so the pros seemed to far outweigh the cons. I also knew that I didn't want my mother-in-law coming to stay for extended time in the early days of bringing our baby home. She had been so controlling and judgmental when she stayed after our first baby that I often hid in my room while she was there, just to protect my energy and have some much needed space.

I raised my concerns with my ex-partner and asked if his mother could just come up for a visit to meet the baby but not stay for weeks at a time, or that she come up later when the baby was a few weeks old, and I'd had time to recover. I mentioned I wanted to hire an au pair to assist us in the first couple of months because we would have two children under two years old and that he could not be around to help because of his work. He immediately disagreed with the au pair and with my concerns about his mother staying with us for too long. He argued with me, stating that his mother would be offended if we got an au pair instead of having her live with us to help for a while. He also admitted he wanted his mother there as well. I really had to stand my ground as I knew he wouldn't even be around as he'd be off working twelve hours a day and I'd be left a prisoner in my home with his mother taking over and criticising my every move in how I parented my own children in my home. On this occasion, and because there was too much at stake, I did not back down and insisted we were getting an au pair. I knew I needed a neutral person in the home as a preventative measure to the escalation of violence when I was in such a vulnerable state while having a newborn. I also knew I would need some support with having a newborn and young toddler to care for 24/7 and was aware that there was not likely to be support from him.

Sure enough though, behind my back and against my wishes, he asked his mother to come and stay for the first few weeks the baby was born while he spent twelve hours a day at work and headed out for his usual after work drinks, leaving me at home with his mother. I was polite and pretended to do things her way to avoid being criticised and to avoid confrontation.

I arranged an au pair to move in for approximately two months at some stage in the newborn phase. Aside from providing an extra pair of hands, it was very comforting and supportive, having a neutral person in the home.

One weekend, when the au pair had a friend come and visit, who was also about 19 years old, I headed out to the shops, leaving our two children home with my ex-partner and her. She told me the following day that her friend had felt really uncomfortable with my ex-partner's behaviour while I was out. She continued explaining that while they were in the spa having a swim, that he came out with his shirt off and started cooking them a BBQ while obviously flirting with her friend to the point it became border line inappropriate. She ended up taking her friend to her bedroom to get away from him, as he wouldn't leave them alone. It didn't bother me in the slightest and although I thought there was likely an element of truth to it, I also brushed it off as young girls over-exaggerating.

A few months went by and the au pair had moved back home overseas. I was in the throes of juggling a young baby and a two-year-old day in day out, while getting up in the night to breastfeed the newborn. I was running on empty, but was doing everything that needed to be done to care for two young children. One evening at about 6:30pm my ex-partner walked in the door after getting home from work and he was on a phone call with his mother as he entered the house. On this occasion, I was trying to get dinner ready before he walked in the door as that was what he expected on arriving home if I was on maternity leave, and I had the baby strapped to me in the carrier crying as they often do at that time of night known as the witching hour. To add to that, our two-year-old didn't want to stay in bed after I had put him down twice already but didn't have the capacity to stay with him because of the baby, and so he was on the kitchen floor crying to be carried by me. It had literally only been about 10 minutes of this chaos, but as my ex-partner walked in the door, my mother-in-law obviously heard crying children. He hung up the phone and assisted in picking up our toddler and getting him back to bed. Although not very relaxing to experience, it was nothing more than a typical evening in a household with a baby and a young toddler with only one person to manage both, and I thought nothing further of it.

Later that evening, as I was cleaning up the kitchen while my ex-partner was taking a shower, I heard him talking on his phone from the bathroom and because he must have been wet from the shower, he had his phone on speaker. He obviously assumed I was still in the kitchen and out of earshot of the conversation that was being had. I admittedly listened to this conversation. His mother was accusingly asking him what I was doing to the children when he got home. His response to this sickened me. He smoothly and calmly told his mother that he had been making sure the children were okay and continued to tell her he had been sleeping in the baby's room at night and getting up to tend to the baby when he wakes. He continued on saying that he doesn't mind doing this and although he is tired, he is more than happy to step up as a father and let me rest, as I wasn't coping well. I was so triggered. My resilience was low from lack of sleep and not to mention the years of stress within the relationship leading up to this time. Not only was it a complete lie in what he had relayed to her, but he had said it so smoothy and with such conviction. He had played himself as a hero while subtly undermining me. I couldn't believe it. Everything had been twisted, re-written in fact to make himself sound like a hero. Her response to him was the straw that broke the camel's back. She critically responded by saying that he should not have to get up in the night as he was working, that I was being lazy and that it had to cease.

I was irate. Not only was it none of her business, but it was completely untrue! I marched into the bathroom and glared at him, clearly indicating that I had just heard the rubbish he had just relayed. He quickly excused himself from the call and hung up. I realised at that moment that he had been pitting me against his mother for ages, planting seeds and triangulating. Not only had he NOT been sleeping in the spare room with the baby, but in fact I had been sleeping in the spare room with the baby for the past month as I was getting too tired walking up and down the hallway multiple times a night to breastfeed. Yes, our baby was still solely breastfeeding, so it was impossible for anyone else to get up in the night to tend to him. It was like he twisted the whole situation to big note himself and put me down to his mother. Of course, her response to this was criticism despite the circumstance not being real. It was so clever on his behalf, as he never blatantly ranted negatively about me to her, but he ever so subtly and manipulatively put himself in a good light while portraying me in a negative light. This behaviour was incredibly effective at triangulating people against each other whilst placing himself in the hero or mediator role where he controls the dynamic.

In reality, he was always off working late, out at after-work drinks, going to leisure sailing weekends and weeks away often while not telling anyone he was going because it would look bad. Yet behind the scenes, he's indicating to his mother and probably others that he is cooking, cleaning, getting up through the night to our newborn baby and more. If it were true, it would have been a smaller and different issue, but with it being so far from the truth and had obviously been going on chronically for ages, it sickened me.

Something clicked or maybe snapped in me at that moment. I had a clear realisation of what I needed to do. In isolation, this event sounded minor and like an overreaction, but in the context of the entire relationship and the state of my nervous system, it was massive that this had occurred.

I went off. I lost my cool. I did not hold back in telling him what I thought of him and his mother. He got defensive and made excuses, saying that I had heard wrong and that he was just telling his mother this so she would leave us alone. The more he denied my experience and the impact this had had on me, the more I fought back to be heard and acknowledged. It got to the stage where I irrationally told him I was going to write to his mother and tell her to stay out of our business. I began writing the text message, and he started begging me not to send it. It was almost like he was panicking about being caught out. I assume this was about not wanting me to ruin the illusional image of himself he portrays to his family, as evidenced in this situation. I sent the message anyway. It was a rant. It was a direct request for her to mind her own business. Some who saw this message said it was fine and was me speaking my truth and setting boundaries. Of course, my ex-partner and his mother spun it to me, being rude and having no right to have a voice in this way. This was the turning point and the beginning of the end for us. It was like I had held on, bottled up, complied, kept quiet for too long and now I was done.

By done, I didn't mean that I felt I could actually leave soon, but more so that I didn't care what his mother thought of me anymore. It was like that fear of criticism and rejection from her was gone in that split second. I felt no respect for her and no respect for my then husband. It was the build-up for years of dealing with this and I was done. I was no longer staying silent. I may as well have stood at the top of a mountain with a megaphone and told the world I was no longer accepting or putting up with these toxic behaviours.

My ex-partner couldn't stand that I was having a voice and putting boundaries in place. He turned on me big time. I realised it was going to be me against his family, even if we stayed together. Deep down, I still didn't feel I had the option to leave at this stage. It felt too big. I was on maternity leave, had two children under two and we were also building a house. A house I never wanted to build or invest in but, as usual, ended up agreeing to keep the peace and try to keep him happy.

We somehow repaired things between us and were amicable over the next few weeks. Life moved forward, and we continued to co-exist within the relationship. Deep down, I was in full-blown survival mode. I felt trapped. I had to block it out and pretend things were fine in order to cope. I decided I needed to seek trauma therapy. By now, and with my big reaction to his mother, I realised I was utterly traumatised from this relationship and the events that had occurred during our time together. I had already tried a psychologist that previous time and recognised that I didn't resonate with talk therapy or counselling approach, so I was looking for something more. I was already a qualified kinesiologist, yet not practicing, so I arranged to have some sessions with an old course colleague whom I had studied with.

It was really helpful in shifting some beliefs that had become embedded through my experiences and also to help regulate my nervous system. Whilst researching about trauma on the internet one evening to help me understand myself and what I was experiencing better, I came across an article on Post Traumatic Stress Disorder (PTSD). I realised the chronic involuntary body twitches (nervous system dysregulation and hypervigilance), insomnia, my big reactions of late (fight survival mode), my shut down and withdrawing from my ex (freeze survival mode) and my life long pattern of people pleasing and changing myself to avoid criticism and rejection (fawn survival mode), was my system displaying many of the symptoms of a highly traumatised person. It made so much sense.

I ended up seeking trauma therapy through a modality called The Richard's Trauma Process (TRTP). It was a series of three sessions. I wasn't the prime candidate to be undertaking this therapy at this stage, as I was still living in a toxic environment, so it was communicated to me that the process may be less effective than if I was out of the toxic environment and had a safe place for my nervous system to heal post therapy. I went ahead with it, anyway.

I definitely felt different after undertaking this process. I carried on with my life and on reflection now, this TRTP process was the key that changed my internal world to see things differently. To see myself differently. It was like a veil was lifted. I was looking out of the fog and not consumed within it. It was very subtle and because I was still living in the toxic environment, I was still experiencing stress, so it was hard to see the level of change it had made.

On reflection, the TRTP process gave me my life back. I saw my ex-partner through a different lens. I felt stronger in myself. I had drive and motivation for life again. The issue was however, that I completely lost respect for my ex-partner. Everything about him irritated me. I felt like rolling my eyes at him constantly. I just saw him as a try hard and full of ego. I began recognising that he knew the behaviours he was choosing to exhibit. The cognitive dissonance I had was gone.

I went back to work after maternity leave shortly after this. I began spending more and more time on myself in doing the things that made me happy. I previously used to stay up watching tv shows I had no interest in just to spend time with my ex-partner. I used to organise date nights or special dinners at home to connect with him more, thinking this was what our relationship needed. I had now reached the stage where I accepted that our relationship would never change. I had tried everything. We were in our new build home by this stage and my ex -partner was distracted for the short while with the novelty of that.

I spent more and more time in my room reading and learning. I was getting up early to meditate. I ceased making an effort to organise date nights. I didn't realise it then, but I had finally given up on him. I no longer felt I needed his connection or strived to move mountains to make this better for us. I even recall telling a good friend at the time over dinner that I knew

I wouldn't be with him forever. I shared this with her when I did as I was feeling quite anxious about this realisation, but I also believed at the time I had no choice but to stay until the children were older.

I continued to notice that I was calmer than usual, although somewhat disconnected, and had really gone inward and withdrawn from the relationship and was doing my own thing. We still did things as a family and I played the game and role, but the best way to describe it - I was detached. I had let go of the need to make it work. Being the type of person he is, he didn't see this change in me as an alarm bell. He took it as an opportunity to get away with more things that served him because I wasn't challenging him on anything anymore.

The COVID pandemic had been active for a while by this stage and everyone was currently on lock down for six weeks. One evening, he approached me with a familiar sweet talking and manipulation tactic he did when he was asking to do something that may not be appropriate or suitable. He said he had put his hand up to go away to work on site for three weeks. That would mean I was going to be home on my own with our two children for that period, while also trying to juggle full-time work and in home lock down. The old me would have gotten upset and stressed out about him selfishly going away when he didn't have to. He was obviously bored at home locked down with his family and thought this was a way out to do something more exciting. If I was being honest, I was actually looking forward to not having him home, as I could relax and do my own thing. Anyone who has had young children in a home lockdown on their own will understand the weight of this statement. Despite this, it was my preference over having him home with us.

When he arrived home, a couple of weeks later, he was acting very sweet and overly affectionate. I realised I felt nothing. I had had a glimpse of what it is like on my own with our two children while trying to maintain a career, and I did it for this brief trial. It was almost easier in a way not having him there, as I didn't have to walk on eggshells or feel the ongoing triggers I experienced when he was around. I also didn't have the pressure of having to keep a perfect house, or have dinner served every night. I could be me and do what felt right in each moment. Was it hard single parenting for this period? Yes, definitely. It wasn't as hard as the relationship itself, though, so my eyes were opening to what I needed to do.

I had the realisation that I would be better off alone than partnered with someone who makes me feel so alone, as that was the loneliest place in the world to be. I know there will be many of you who can relate to the overwhelming sense of loneliness that comes from the irreparable sense of disconnect from your partner. The realisation that you will never be seen, heard, validated, respected and cared for by this person. That knowing that this person who is supposed to have your back and support you no matter what, simply doesn't and never will. Realising that you carried the bulk of the relationship, sacrificed so much, and it was never enough and would never be enough. Trying desperately to make it work and seeing that it was always to no avail. The realisation that whatever you did, didn't do, changed, altered, adapted, you still always fell short of any meaningful change. The realisation that the life you had tried to create, hoped for, had envisioned, and had been promised was never within reach. That you were sold a lie and were used. And with all this, you still feel stuck, as if you have no option but to stay. This is the loneliest place to be. And leaving this place, although an obvious choice, is anything but obvious or easy when you are in it.

If you take away anything from this book, let it be consideration to this confronting yet necessary message. A message I wished I knew and believed much earlier than I did. A message that could have saved me from the horrendous lessons that eventually landed me with this solid realisation. For those who are truly in a genuine narcissistic relationship with someone who uses coercive control, or any form of domestic violence, and who fails to seek genuine help for change, there is little chance at true happiness if you stay. Your life will probably only get worse. Your health can and will deteriorate and your mental health will continue to suffer. That's just the impact on you, but your children will be exposed to abuse one hundred percent of the time while you stay, whether directly witnessed or indirectly through the traumatic impacts it has on you.

What they see at home will solely shape their modelling for love and relationships. This will be their compass for love and their belief of what a relationship looks like that they will carry into their own adulthood. While leaving is hard and staying feels even harder, when you really break it down, there is no other choice. There is no other sustainable option but to choose you, and that means choosing hard. This is not to judge those that choose to stay. It is completely understandable why people choose to stay. But you truly cannot live any form of quality life under these conditions. Everyone will suffer the long term consequences.

The only way to heal and eventually thrive is to extract yourself from the environment that is making you sick and poisoning everything it touches. There was a time when I thought I needed to stay for our children. I thought I would ruin their lives by leaving. I didn't believe I could do it on my own. It wasn't until the confronting realisation landed that I wouldn't be around to care for them long term if I stayed and that would ruin their life far more than having parents live in different homes.

THE DEPTH OF HER SURVIVAL

I also realised that they had been witness to the abuse in various ways since birth, and although too young to comprehend what was occurring, as they became old enough to communicate and comprehend right from wrong, they were caught in the middle of it. I knew this was far more damaging to them than the changes divorce would bring. It's difficult to leave. It will be one of the hardest things you will ever have to do. But it will be worth it, and it may be the only chance at establishing health and happiness in your lifelong term.

This is not intended at pressuring or shaming those who choose to stay long term. It is the sharing of my experience. It is what I have seen through so many of my clients in similar situations. It is what can be taken away from the evidenced research on these types of relationships and people with these disorders. If you truly know for certain you are in a form of domestic violence relationship with a disordered person, whether that be emotionally or physically, then seek the support to really understand what it is you are in and look into the options available to move you to safety, stability and freedom if that is what you desire.

I have helped many people in my work to build themselves up to have the strength to leave if that's the path they choose, as well as to manage their wellbeing while they still choose to stay. It's crucial to have the support through the aftermath of leaving if that's the path you decide to take. Although the post-separation period may be traumatic and prolonged, there is light at the end of the tunnel. There is a way. There is support available, and you don't have to do it alone.

Divorce doesn't break up families. Abuse and betrayal do.

CHAPTER 10

THE COURAGE TO JUMP

People are often afraid of being alone when the actual fear should be about having the wrong people as company.

A few days after my ex-partner returned home from the work trip, he told me he had to go back out to site again to work for a few days, but this time it was over an extended weekend. This was very suspicious as I knew for a fact, he never has to go to site on a weekend for his role as an office employee. I also knew that he would never have to do a routine site trip so soon after arriving home from the last. I knew in that moment that he was lying to me, but I didn't know why or what the real reason was for him needing to go away on this upcoming occasion. The old me would have reacted, panicked and challenged him, trying to seek safety in the connection. The current and detached version of me simply didn't care. I was quite tired from life and having somewhat let go of our relationship energetically and emotionally in recent times, I did not care enough to question him.

I was thinking how much more pleasant it would be to have the house to myself again. He left on this trip and when he came home the following week, I was met with an almost slimy attentiveness and over the top affection toward me. It repelled me. I felt nothing. I continued to play families the best I could and went through the motions of co-existing as a couple. I didn't know how else to live life at this stage inside this dynamic. I was still somewhat in denial about what I needed to do and avoiding the realisation that I had to leave the relationship.

The following morning, we took the children for a walk to the park. Our son had just turned three and wanted to take his scooter instead of his bike, but my ex-partner insisted he wanted him to take his bike. Our son became upset as he wanted his scooter not the bike, so I stepped in and suggested we let him take his scooter and explained it was about our children enjoying themselves, not about us. He didn't like that I stood up to him, but begrudgingly accepted. On the way down to the park, our three-year-old had some frustration about his scooter rolling onto the grass around the corners. My ex-partner became agitated and suddenly ripped our son's scooter out from under him, and threw it aggressively onto the footpath, while swearing and barking blame at me for the fact we had his scooter. Now, it wouldn't have mattered if our son was on his bike or scooter, as the same thing would have happened while he was learning to balance and ride. My ex-partner was having a tantrum about not getting his own way and projected that onto me and his own son. This episode was not only intimidating, but it caused tension for what was supposed to be a nice morning outing, however we continued on.

When we got to the park, my ex-partner told me to go across the road to the café and get us both a coffee. He could see I didn't bring my phone or purse, so without thinking, he unlocked his phone, handed it to me and told me to use Apple Pay. As soon as he handed his phone over to me, I saw a startled look appear on his face and he tried to take the phone back and made an excuse that he would go over and get the coffees. I absolutely saw and felt his reaction and knew he was hiding something. Before he had the opportunity to take the phone back, I casually turned and walked off. I kept my thumb on the screen to avoid it password locking again.

While at the café, I felt like a criminal. I knew I had to look. This was my life, and I was trapped in a loveless marriage that I didn't know how to get out of. I made the choice to look at his phone. My heart was pounding through my chest. I knew it was wrong to invade someone's privacy. I also knew I needed answers and a way forward. Sure enough, within five seconds, I'm looking at a set of female boobs, and they weren't mine. There were months' worth of ongoing private messages, with personal photos, videos, and daily chat with an attractive brunette woman. I don't know why I was shocked, as the signs had been there for a long time. I quickly grabbed our coffees and headed back to the park, and pretended nothing had happened. I didn't say anything. Partially because our children were there, and it wasn't the right time, and partially because I felt so guilty. I had checked his phone and didn't know how to explain that. He had changed his password to his phone about six months prior, so it made sense.

We used to know each other's phone password to play music at home, but one occasion a few months prior, when he asked me to change the music, I wasn't able to as his password had been changed. I asked him about it as it was odd, and he brushed it off and made sure he changed his own music moving forward from that time. I was definitely suspicious, but I didn't see the point in harping on about it.

So now I had seen more evidence of infidelity and having an affair, and everything started piecing together. He didn't need to go away to site for work over that previous weekend at all. Wherever he had gone, it was to be there because this woman was there. Snippets of evidence related to this would come out about two years later in documentation related to our separation legal proceedings. All the late nights he spent staying upstairs in the office until midnight. The changing of the phone password. The unusual work trips away. I realised I had to say something. I also realised this was my opportunity to escape the relationship.

We were due to go to a friend's place that evening for a barbecue. I didn't want to go with all this going on, but I also didn't want to stay home with him, so I planned to go, nevertheless. He was outside in the yard while the children were inside watching cartoons. I took the opportunity to have a conversation with him outside of earshot of the children. I approached him and he had no idea what I was about to drop. I calmly and firmly went straight to the point. I firstly stated that I know it was wrong and confessed that I looked at his phone this morning when I was getting coffee. I saw him get nervous. I continued saying I know he has been having an affair, and I told him about the naked photos and the six months of private messages from the brunette female. He immediately went on the attack. First telling me I have trust issues and that I had no right to check his phone. He continued without a breath, saying my mother has messed me up and that's why I have trust issues and I need to stop making things up and overreacting. Gaslighting. I ignored his deflection this time and advised him that despite his belief on trust issues being the root cause of this issue, there was still a woman who had her boobs on his phone that morning along with other naked photos and intimate daily messages over the past six months.

In his anger and panic, he slipped up. The next sentence that came out was like a giant foot he may as well have put straight in his mouth. While claiming they were just friends and she was a friend of a colleague from work, he followed on by stating that there had been heaps of other messages between them, but he had deleted them. I stared blankly at him, trying to work out why he would incriminate himself even further, until I realised it had been an attempt to downplay their interactions, but ultimately ended in disclosing he had been deleting and hiding conversations along the way for much longer. He immediately realised what he had said and stopped.

The blame and put downs continued to come in hard and fast and I was suddenly the focus with him, stating I need to get help for my issues. It was a typical case of DARVO – Deny, Attack, Reverse, Victim and Offender[1]. I was only to learn what this tactic was through my later experience with him in the Domestic Violence and Family Court systems. Being educated on this form of psychological abuse and experiencing it repeatedly through the legal process gave me firsthand insight and experience into this common tactic executed by abusers when they are caught out. It is aimed at trying to flip the narrative to paint themselves as a victim and place unwarranted and completely false allegations on a true victim in an attempt to re-write history. He was highly skilled at this tactic. He would use this tactic extensively during our legal process and it worked every time in triggering me into a big reaction trying to defend myself. All the while, the real issue of what we were arguing about, his actions and behaviour, was forgotten and deflected from.

Because our children were at home, I could stay somewhat calm from his attack and projection, and I shut the conversation down. I went back inside and started getting ready to go to our friend's place. Our children were around once he came back inside, so nothing further was said, although I could have cut the tension with a knife. I could sense he was a ticking time bomb on the inside, and I was feeling anxious about what was to come.

Once we arrived at our friend's house for the barbeque, we pretended everything was fine and were distracted by socialising and mixing with our friends. Of course, it was still on the forefront of my mind, but there's nothing I could do except for pretend that everything was okay and try to enjoy the evening. A short while into the night after he has been mingling with the other husbands outside, he approached me with a loving gesture and put his arms around me, gave me a familiar puppy dog look as if to show he was sorry. This would usually have worked on me and had many times before, but what I knew was that being around other couples and experiencing the buzz and connection from socializing with friends, masks the underlying issues and as soon as we are away from socializing with others, the true colours and issues return.

This time was different. I had clarity that I needed to leave, and imminently. A little later in the night, when it was getting past our children's bedtime, I suggested we head home. He said he would be ready soon. About an hour later, our three-year-old son was playing with some toys on a mat with one of the other children his age, when the two of them suddenly started fighting over a toy they both wanted. In a split second, our son opened his mouth wide and was going in for a bite to the other child's arm in an act of frustration. My ex-partner saw this unfolding and launched across the room with a beer still in his hand, pushed our son at force across the room so hard that he slammed into the kitchen bench. Our son was crying and wide eyed, obviously scared and in shock. I rushed over to comfort him, but my ex-partner got there first and picked him up. I could tell he was about to lose his cool. The fact he knew others may have witnessed this would have been a huge issue for him. I tried to take our son from him to comfort him and to just get him away from his father while he was so erratic and flighty. This resulted in a tug a war of our child, which felt awful, but I could finally take him and get him settled while my ex-partner was barking orders that we needed to get home. He was mumbling under his breath and blaming our three-year-old son for everything that had just unfolded. The car trip home was dead silent. No-one spoke a word. I could see my ex-partner tapping his fingers at speed on the steering wheel and his eyes glaring ahead of him. He was enraged.

At home, after I put the children to bed, I quietly told him we needed to talk in the morning about our separation. I then went outside and sat on the front lawn. I was torn up inside and in anguish over not knowing the way forward. I was frightened at his demeanour, and I knew he was going to completely lose it if I insisted on separating. I could sense his internal rage and dysregulation building. He was a ticking time bomb. As I sat on the front lawn that evening in the dark, I looked up and noticed there was a full moon. I was feeling so desperate and so alone in this decision that I knew I had to follow through on this time. I looked up at this powerful moon in the night sky and pleaded for help from whoever or whatever was out there. I felt like I was standing on the edge of a cliff and was about to jump off without a parachute.

That night, my ex-partner slept in the spare room. In the morning I woke up to an email from him. It was harsh and full of emotion stating that I was ruining his life and our children's life by leaving, and that I needed to take accountability for how much I have ruined our relationship. It was quite the trigger to read this. To add to this highly activating email, he continued to say that we were having a lovely evening when our son "assaulted" his friend and he had to step in to discipline him. He admitted that pushing him across the room was too much, but excused it with the claim that it was our son's fault for assaulting his friend. This projection of blame on our three-year-old and the complete lack of accountability for his own behaviour had me seeing red. It's one thing to psychologically abuse me as an adult partner for years with this pattern of behaviour, but the minute he began doing the same to our own child, it was like the mamma bear protector came out with full force. In that moment, I made a pack to myself that no way in hell would I allow this man to do what he has done to me to our children. They were only still so little and the projection and blame shifting had begun already, so my concerns about what it was going to be like when they got older and when calling things out or trying to speak up to him were very real. Not in my living days was I about to stand by submissively and watch this occur to our own children. I suddenly had the courage to jump head first right off that cliff I had been standing on the edge of for so long now. The band aid needed to be ripped off right here and now. I went and approached my ex-partner and calmly yet firmly re-affirmed that we were done. That our relationship was over. We were separating and there was nothing that could stop me or change my mind this time. I continued in advising that we needed to work amicably to get it done quickly and smoothy for the least impact on our children. The courage and confidence that I entered this cliff jump with soon dwindled and dissipated with what was about to unfold next.

CHAPTER 11

IF I CAN'T HAVE YOU I WILL DESTROY YOU

After telling my ex-partner that we were done, he completely lost his shit.

I was called every name under the sun and accused of ruining his life. I was told that it was my family and I that were the issue, and that he has done nothing to deserve this. The rage and utter dysregulation that was being projected out and towards me had me shut down in fear. I timidly tried to tell him to keep his voice down as the children were in the next room. He got louder and more volatile. I said nothing. I didn't speak. I was frozen with fear. I was looking at the ground, trying not to do anything that might tip him right over the edge.

I glanced up and was heartbroken to see our three-year-old standing at the doorway wide eyed with a panicked look on his face. I gave him a softened expression of reassurance the best way I could with my ex-partner standing between me and the doorway our son was peering out of. Our son suddenly changed his tone and, in an authoritarian voice with a big frown, yelled out to us, "*Stop it! Stop fighting!*" He didn't move from his doorway position, but he had quite the presence. My ex-partner didn't even flinch or turn around to acknowledge him. He just kept on with his aggressive rant towards me at full volume. I finally spoke up and firmly told him to stop and be quiet as our son was watching. He threw his arms in the air and swore some more before turning around and storming off, right past our son without even acknowledging him, and down the stairs out of the front door. As the door slammed behind him, our three-year-old immediately ran over to me asking, *"did daddy hurt you?"*

I forced a smile and reassured him in an attempted casual voice everything was fine and he had nothing to worry about.

My nervous system was shot. My heart had constant palpitations that wouldn't stop. My brain felt fried. I couldn't think straight or string a sentence together. I was becoming increasingly concerned about what he was going to do next. He was volatile and off the charts with rage at me for pushing forward with our separation. He was gone for about half the day when he suddenly arrived home. I didn't know what to expect. He approached me in the home, still in a heightened state, but somewhat calmer than when he left. He told me he had called Beyond Blue, which is a suicide hotline, while he was out and shared that they suggested he was suffering with depression and continued saying the consultant on the phone indicated she was quite concerned about his wellbeing. Now normally I would have immense compassion for anyone sharing their mental health challenges. On this occasion, it didn't feel right. It was his energy or something he was giving off, almost as if he was trying to make me feel sorry for him and manipulate my feelings. I was still feeling extremely threatened. I acknowledged what he had just shared and continued by saying I hope he gets the support he needs. I said we need to address the elephant in the room and work out a plan for our separation, reaffirmed it was happening, and reiterated our need to do it amicably for the children.

He completely flew off the handle again. The yelling abuse at me started all over again. This time I panicked and said I would head out for a while to give him some space. I contacted a friend and asked if she was free to meet me at a local café and we arranged to meet there. I was so torn about leaving our children with him in this state. I also knew I was what was aggravating him and knew I needed to leave to diffuse the situation. He wouldn't stop yelling and ranting, and our children were witnessing everything. I simply said that I was heading out for a while to give him some space and began heading down the stairs to the front door. I didn't even approach the children to say goodbye as I was so concerned he was about to explode at me, so I knew I needed to leave immediately to diffuse the situation. My attempt to leave enraged him even more. He was barking at me that I had to stay and talk about it. It was all dominance and control and so much aggression. There was no way a productive conversation was his intentions. I continued to leave the house. He ran down the stairs after me and stood in front of the door, blocking me from leaving. I was silent. Internally panicked but trying not to give my fear away.

I turned and went through the garage door instead and made my way to the car to get in it, which was parked in the driveway. He came around in front of me and blocked me from getting into the car. He was still going off at me verbally. I was dead silent. Petrified, but not wanting to let him know just how frightened

I actually was. I told him to get out of my way and to stop bullying me. He leaned right up into my face, still blocking me from getting past and said, *"go on, hit me"*.

I just stood there frozen. I was petrified he was going to become violent. Instinct kicked in and I reached on top of his head to where his sunglasses were resting and I pulled them off his head and threw them as far as I could behind him as a decoy. When he turned his head to look after his sunglasses, I quickly ran around him, jumped into the car, locked the doors and wound up the window that was currently down. He raced to the window of the car and pressed his body firmly up against the car, still raving and ranting at me about leaving. The window closed just in time. I pressed the remote for the electric gate that was about two metres behind the car to open at the end of the short driveway. He was still right up in my window, hurling abuse at me. I reversed the car out of the driveway and headed off to meet my friend at the café.

My mind was racing. I was so concerned about our children left back at home with him in his state. I questioned if I should have attempted to load them in the car with me, but knew there was no way he would have allowed that to happen and they would only have been put in harm's way by attempting to do that. I convinced myself I had done the only thing I could in that situation by leaving to diffuse the situation until I figured out what I needed to do. I couldn't think of a solution or a safe way forward. I met my friend at the café and left my sunglasses on to hide my emotional state from passers-by. I diplomatically shared that things were not good at home. While I was there, I suddenly received a photo of my two children from an unknown number. I did not know who it was or where they were. A text message came through shortly after stating that our children were fine and if I needed extra time to head to the hospital with my ex-partner, then the children could stay there as long as needed. It ended up being the neighbours about six doors up on our street who I had only met on a couple of occasions and barely knew. I did not know what my ex-partner had said to them or why he had asked them to have our children. I immediately left the café to head over to collect our children.

I walked into their home after they answered the door, not really knowing what to expect, as I didn't know what they had been told. They seemed as confused as I was and said that my ex-partner seemed to be in immense pain and had asked them to look after the boys while he went to the hospital. I immediately thought he had a mental breakdown and was self-admitting, but it seemed odd he would call the neighbours and not contact me to tell me to come home to care for the children. No matter what was going on between us, I thought that our children's welfare would always be put first.

After taking our children back home, my three-year-old told me the ambulance had come. I felt overwhelmingly anxious about what my ex-partner had plotted or was up to. It didn't add up.

What I was about to uncover was that he had calculatedly and intentionally contacted a third person, our neighbours, to create a witness portfolio of evidence for his disturbing, vindictive and calculated plan he was irrationally executing as revenge in attempt to control me for trying to leave him. I had an idea to check our security camera at the front door to see if I could see what unfolded. Sure enough, not long after I drove out of the driveway from home, you can see my ex-partner walking in and out of the house and garage for about ten minutes, pacing around, obviously enraged. A short while later, the neighbours up the road are seen to arrive and take our children with them just as an ambulance turns up at the house and puts my ex-partner on a stretcher. I was mortified! What was this dramatic and erratic situation that he was creating involving other people and exposing our children to, whilst leaving them with people they barely knew while he was well aware I was only five minutes up the road?

He had worked out that I was actually leaving the relationship for good. This was the first time his intimidation, followed by manipulation, had not worked in luring me back in to agree to give our relationship another go. He knew I meant it this time, and that I was going to follow through. The lack of control this created in him sent him into a complete dysregulated spiral, where vindictive and calculated intent took over him. If he couldn't own me or keep me under his control, he was going to destroy me at all costs. It was soon to become his obsession in the immediate years that followed in our post-separation period.

I still didn't know what was going on or why he had called an ambulance to go to the hospital. I was full of panic about what the next steps forward were to get out of this danger zone I could sense I was in. I saw a side of him I had only seen glimpses of before during the relationship, but it never lasted and was eventually followed by an apology and the return of some normality. This time it was like he went to an extreme level, and I knew my life was in danger while he was in this state. However, I did not actually realise the depth of danger I was truly in. He was about to show himself to be far more calculated, malicious, and vindictive than I had ever seen him before, and well beyond my comprehension of what he was capable of.

What he had planned to bring me down for daring to leave him was not only pure evil, but was a criminal offense. I was not ready or equipped to deal with or cope with what was unfolding behind the scenes and the level my life was about to be dragged down to by this man who was claiming to love me and didn't want me to leave. I was soon to learn it was never love but a deep-rooted disorder that was obsessed with having control over me. I was nothing more than a mere possession that he believed he now owned.

Later that night, I heard him come through the front door. He walked in on crutches, looked at me, and went to the spare room. I locked myself in our bedroom that night and tried to get some sleep. I had to be at work at 7am the next morning so was up trying to get the children ready for daycare and would have to do the usual rush out the door to get on the road to work. He intercepted me at the front door, blocked me from exiting and unleashed on me all over again. Accusing me of ruining his life. Projecting onto me that there is something wrong with me and I'm the problem in our relationship. I stated I had to get to work and eventually left. He was ranting and yelling after me as I was driving off. I had to block it out. I had a massive day at work ahead and I needed to focus. I also reflected and had noticed he was no longer on his crutches that morning and already had his work shoes on and was walking around just fine. I was confused about why he came home on crutches the night before, but didn't have the time or capacity to wonder about that and just let it go.

My day at work was full on and I was running on adrenaline, trying to appear normal and keep on top of the intensity of my workload. I had not long sat down to begin a three-hour management meeting and was about to report on the monthly performance of my team when a text message came through to my phone. It was from my ex-partner. I glanced down to scan it briefly. It stopped me in my tracks. My hands began trembling under the table in the boardroom. My heart was pounding through my chest. I felt like I was going to have a panic attack. I didn't, however. I held it in, suppressed it and tried to appear normal to my work team. I briefly said my bit when it was my turn to present to the group. I was on complete auto pilot. The text message I unexpectedly received read as this:

It's with a heavy heart that I send you this. I have reported to the police about what happened yesterday, and the police will contact you to issue you a report. You can do this at the station. You need to get help to address your issues and accept them. I don't understand why you can't accept and be sorry that you ran over my foot. All I want is a happy family with you. There is hope, but only if you address things with me. I will not be home tonight. I was fearful that I would lose the boys. I had to protect myself against those threats. If the shoe were on the other foot, you would have done the same.

The message continued on with this utter crazy making content. It was not only a complete lie, distortion and fabrication of the events but also a direct admission he reported a false allegation against me to police with intent to taint my character and try to advantage himself in our parenting matters.

I was terrified. I couldn't comprehend or believe what he had done. Not long after, I received a text from the local police saying I had to report to them before 5pm that day. This was followed by a phone call I received from my then best friend saying her husband had just called her because my ex-partner had contacted him asking if he could come and stay with them for a week because he wasn't able to stay at our home. My friend was initially uncomfortable with this plan of my ex-partner staying with them and acknowledged I was her friend and that it was strange to have my husband stay with them when I needed her support. I would soon discover this to be short-lived once he set to work on his smear campaign and mission to isolate me from my closest supports. He wanted to stay with my best friend to influence her first and isolate me from this avenue of support that he knew was my strongest backing at this stage.

I finished my work day, rushed to collect our children from daycare, and headed straight to the police station. I had to take our children to the police station. I had no other option at this time of the evening. Deep down I knew that what he had reported was all rubbish and a lie that would have to work itself out, but all I could feel was sheer terror and was crippled with fear and disempowerment at what he had just done. I walked into the police station and stated that I was advised to report there after a false claim had been submitted on me. I tried to explain that it was all made up and did not happen. The officer handed me my ex-partner's report that the police had put together on his behalf, based on his story, and told me I had to sign the report to accept it and would then be issued with a Domestic Violence Protection Order (DVO) against me to protect my ex-partner. They advised me that if I did not agree, I needed to present to the Domestic and Family Violence Magistrate's Court the following Tuesday for a contested hearing. I was treated like a criminal, as if I was guilty without even being asked my side, and without being interviewed or any evidence at all being looked at. It was currently based on my ex-partner's word alone. It was my first insight into the corrupt and unjust legal system and how this very system enables abusers to maintain control and execute further abuse. This was a case of DARVO at its finest.

That night I blasted my ex-partner over text telling him I'd see him in court the following week with my years of evidence of his abuse and that I would put this blame back where it belonged. He spent the evening at my friend's house, trying to convince them of his narrative while trying to bully me over text into just accepting the report instead of going to court. There was no way I was accepting something completely false, and I knew the only option I had was to fight for the truth. When my ex-partner worked out I would not be intimidated into accepting it. He changed his tone. By the next day he was full of remorse, turning up at our home in tears and apologising stating how badly he had treated me and that I didn't deserve it. He was so truly sorry, or so I thought. I fell into the old pattern of feeling sorry for him, wanting harmony, and just wanting the situation to resolve and go away. He set to work to have the false report removed. He was told he wasn't able to now that it had been reported to the police, and the process was underway. He wrote to the court, he wrote to the police, all to have it removed. Nothing worked. Their process was strict and tight. We had to present to court. He became anxious. I thought he was worried about me and what he had done to me in this false allegation. I was later to discover he was only concerned about himself and getting himself off this, as it would end up being shown as an act of perjury, which is a criminal offense.

My stress levels were through the roof. I had a twelve-month-old baby and a three-year-old, working full time while trying to navigate a separation, and now had to prepare to go to court at short notice as an offender. I was terrified of this man. I couldn't believe he stooped to this level. In his remorse he admitted in tears he thought I reported him all those years ago for the assaults to have them on record and he was worried about losing rights to his children, so admitted he did this false report to level things out by putting a claim on me. He continued admitting he didn't realise the process was that it would have to go to court. He thought it would just be a black mark against my name on record. I felt like I was living in a horror movie.

My life and future were in his hands. He continued to tell me he would get "us" out of this and was acting as if we were a team that needed to work together. I tried to get myself a lawyer, and he shut that down with manipulation, telling me the court said it could all be sorted easily. I was a fool for listening to him. I did not know the process involved or the severity of what this all meant. He was sweet as pie leading up to court day. He wrote me an affidavit and turned up at my house, saying I had to sign it so he could submit it for me to have the case removed. I couldn't think straight. I couldn't comprehend what was actually going on. I signed it in desperation to have this all over. I felt there was no choice but to trust him and let him try to have it removed.

On the morning we had to present to court, I was in complete panic mode. My nervous system was on full alert. I insisted on reviewing the documents he had taken charge of providing to the court on my behalf. I suddenly noticed that he had changed the wording on the affidavit I had signed, making it read that I had never been in any harm and that this situation was a simple misunderstanding. Prior to signing, I had insisted that my affidavit state his allegations were false, because they were, and he had agreed to this and changed the text to say just this. Somehow, my signed version now said otherwise. It was not only fraud, but I did not want to be in a position where I had signed under oath something that could come back and be twisted onto me. It was too late to write another affidavit, and I panicked. I was cursing him in the street in utter disbelief at his dishonesty, and I began running around the local area trying to find a lawyer's office who I could engage in last minute to help me. He followed me, not letting me out of his sight and ramping up the manipulation in telling me he had my back and I didn't need a lawyer. I wasn't able to find a lawyer at short notice and there was nothing I could do. I knew I couldn't trust him.

The time came when we had to present for our court hearing, so I had to just accept things as they were and hope for the best. When we were called separately into the courtroom, I discovered the police prosecutor represented him and I was unrepresented and sat alone. It was horrible. The court hearing began as I sat alone and terrified on the aggressor side of the stand while my ex-partner, the true perpetrator, sat represented by the police on the side of the victim. The magistrate opened the case. The police officer read out my ex-partner's report and accusations. They gave him an opportunity to speak, to which he tried to say it was a misunderstanding and eventually admitted under oath and on record that he made the claim falsely against his wife in a moment of emotion after realising he was losing his family. I still have this audio recording of the court transcript to this day. The magistrate stopped him immediately after these words left his mouth and advised him that what he had done was perjury and could result in prison time. I felt a sense of relief wave over me as this unfolded. The magistrate asked him if he believed I ran over his foot. He responded by saying his foot was run over, but there was no way I could have known. He then continued by saying it was because he put his foot intentionally under the car wheel when I was trying to leave and that I would have had no idea that it happened. The magistrate paused to think and then said to the prosecuting police officer who was representing my ex-partner that he wanted to dismiss the case and have it removed.

What the prosecuting police officer did next shocked me and caught me off guard. It didn't make any sense. The prosecuting police officer challenged the magistrate and said that he didn't believe it should be wiped and suggested that good behaviour be placed on me for six months and if no further police involvement was sought, then the case be dismissed at the next court hearing that would be set for the end of the six months. The magistrate said it sounded reasonable, and that is what he ordered.

I was shocked. I did not get asked a single question. I did not get a single opportunity to have a voice or share my side or how this had made me feel. Not an ounce of evidence was looked at. It was like I was invisible. The outcome was that I had to be on good behaviour for six months where there was no further police involvement and then we had to present back to court, and if all had gone smoothly with no further issues, the case would be wiped clean and dismissed. I was devastated by this outcome. I was later to learn the police pushing for this was completely political and a covering up approach for them. They had not done the due diligence in investigating this case and had gotten it wrong, out of incompetency and complacency. They now had to act as if the risk was real to cover themselves.

I was innocent and was in fact the person who was actually at risk of harm, and I was held to these conditions which gave my ex-partner complete power and control over me and my life until the case was closed in six months' time. To have this injustice occur during an already stressful life period added a whole other layer of trauma to the process. My ex-partner seemed relieved that the perjury aspect didn't go any further and that the truth about his domestic violence history didn't get a chance to be voiced by me. He held onto his remorse towards me for the next few days, and I was holding onto hope the six months would go smoothly. I couldn't have been more wrong.

It wasn't long before my ex-partner soon worked out that he was in the position of power and that I was going to need to behave like a puppet on the string as one more report from him to police, even if it was another false one, would land me with a

Temporary Domestic Violence Protection Order (TDVO) placed on me until we had a trial date set. I couldn't even feel the anger that I knew had every right to be there. I was just terrified.

Disempowered. Exhausted. My nervous system was completely fried. I didn't know how to keep up caring for our young children on my own, working full time and dealing with all of this. It was too much. A couple of days after he got away with this perjury and false allegations and walked away with me in a position where he could pull the strings, his remorse faded and his controlling behaviour returned with a vengeance. He had thought that him getting this removed and not progressing with his false allegations would result in me being so grateful and walking straight back into his arms for his good deed. When he worked out that I wanted nothing to do with him and continued to demand space, he became obsessive with trying to control me. The remorse he had shown leading up to the court date had dwindled fast. It was like all the apologies and begging for forgiveness was all a show to manipulate me into not speaking up in court about the truth of our past and making a formal complaint about the blatant false allegation and perjury that he had committed.

Over the next six months while I needed to be on good behaviour and ensure no other police involvement occurred between us, despite him being the one to drag them into it in the first place, he was like a yo-yo of cycles of extreme control, blaming and degrading me, mixed with attempts to manipulate me through fake care, acts of "love" and periods of no contact.

When he was out on weekends doing his own thing, I had peace and didn't hear from him. When he knew I was having my me time after we eventually established for the children to spend time with him every second weekend, he would bombard me with messages, phone calls and stalking my every move. I discovered he had set up a camera at the front door that he told me was disabled, only to discover he was watching my every move. Every time he saw one of my friends visit, like clockwork, he would contact their husbands to say hi within minutes of them arriving at my home. It was a traceable pattern and was one sign that gave away his stalking behaviours via this security camera. He targeted the husbands of my friends he saw visiting me. It was like he needed to get to every avenue of support he could see I had. He would catch up with my friends' husbands and subtly twist the story and paint me as the problem. This smear campaign involved not only blatant attacks on my character. He also adopted an ever so clever and subtle approach of acting as if he was concerned about me, expressing his sadness that he was losing his family, showing fake remorse for his part in our issues and then dropping a huge fabrication in that I had made him behave in certain ways. He played the victim, and he was very good at pulling on people's heartstrings to make them feel sympathy towards him.

I had to set very firm boundaries with him about him coming to the family home where the children and I were living. He had been allowing himself access and had refused to sell the home to allow me the means to move into a different home and move on. I was stuck there until we completed our settlement. He had been renting a home of his own for quite a few months and had taken with him anything he pleased. I desperately needed to feel safe in my own living space and him coming in and entering without consent was causing me so much fear and anxiety that I had to insist he was not to come to the home.

During the six-month police enforced good behaviour order, I did not want him coming anywhere near me and needed my space.

He almost too easily agreed that he would honour my wishes and not come to the house. One afternoon not long after, I came home from work slightly earlier than usual. I pulled into the driveway to find him walking out of my home with an arm full of items hidden under a towel. He had no other way out except to walk right by the car and I wound down the window to engage with him about why he was breaking into my locked home that we agreed he would not attend. I felt myself freeze up and instead of demanding he leave, or having courage to report him, or even asking him to show me what he had just taken from the home, I instead appeased and didn't want to rock the boat or ruin the chance of continuing towards an amicable dynamic between us.

He put on the sweetest apology and stated he didn't want to disturb me at work, so he just quickly had to go in and get a pizza tray he needed. I said nothing. There was an obvious bulk of items under the towel, and he was clearly trying to manipulate me to thinking it was an innocent situation. I let it go, and he left. This situation occurred yet again a few weeks later, but this time I saw him enter when viewing security on the camera recording. The six month period leading up to the follow up court case was a series of moments of peace and cooperation and the other extreme of full-blown arguments and him tormenting me non-stop until I would react. It was truly awful. I couldn't get a break to rest or process anything that had happened. I was working full-time, spending evenings and every ounce of spare time caring for our young children and had zero time for recuperation.

I finally had a weekend to myself where he took the children to stay with him. I had a girl's weekend away planned but kept that quiet to myself. Like clockwork, the moment I arrived at my weekend away location, I received a phone call from him. He was sweet as pie and asking me where I was going this weekend.

I thought it was strange, as I never told him I was going away. He said he was ringing to tell me how much he loved me and hoped I could have a relaxing weekend. He then said he was so worried I was going to meet someone else and sweetly said he wanted to keep working on changing so he could be the partner I deserved. It was really intense and over the top, and I wanted to enjoy my own time without him bombarding me. When I arrived home the next day, my son asked me how my trip away was. I was shocked. I had never told my son I was going away anywhere. I realised then that my ex-partner had worked out where I was going and had needed to push himself into my awareness, as he couldn't handle me having a good time without him. He knew I had been having such a difficult and exhausting time since our separation and the fact I was doing something for me this weekend, it was like he couldn't handle it and had to make himself the focus of my weekend. I would later discover exactly how he knew where I had gone. It would become known that he had tapped himself into all of my electronic devices before he left, and he was tracking me through my location on my phone. When I left our hometown for our weekend away, he could see where I was and he needed to regain control by ringing me.

Over the next few months, there were times I had peace and didn't hear from him. I knew he was out dating women and partying it up. I didn't care. I thought the sooner he found another woman, the sooner he would let up on the control and the sooner I would be free to close out this chapter and move on. I couldn't have been more wrong.

As we approached the six months and the follow up court date closed in, so did his cooperation and behaviour that appeared to be amicable and indicate he wanted harmony and resolve, which is what I desperately wanted. I had been pushing hard to have our parenting and property matters completed and put into legal orders so we could move forward, re-establish stability in life and put our focus on co-parenting our children. After months of his games, stalling and resistance, he suddenly agreed to mediate and although an extremely stressful process, we came to an agreement on all our separation settlement matters and it was written up into a contract by him and signed by us both.

The sense of relief I felt was enormous. I thought it was all done and over and we could now move on. We both agreed to having it put into legal orders to ensure it was secure and he asked me to arrange this. He had me convinced and believing our matters were agreed upon and resolved and we were going to execute the plan and have them legally binding. This would later be a complete manipulation to ensure I went into the court hearing, feeling like we had closure and believing there was no threat moving forward and, therefore, I wouldn't speak up about his domestic violence history.

Going into the follow up court date, all I wanted was to put it behind us. I thought because we finalised our parenting and property matters that the threat was reduced, and the worst was behind us. I was soon to be thrown into a world where this man, who was currently claiming to be remorseful, promising we were on the road to being amicable for our children, would show me the depth of darkness of who was really lurking behind the mask.

CHAPTER 12

THE MONSTER UNDER THE MASK

One of the hardest things a woman can do is to leave a coercive, controlling relationship... until they enter the family court and its supporting systems. It's like escaping the beast only to find his master waiting for you - Renee Izammbard

One thing I have learnt through my experience but also through supporting others who are going through a separation with an abusive person, is that it is very easy to tell who the true victim is in a relationship once you have the knowledge and experience of looking through a trauma-informed lens. The actual victim will be broken, reactive, anxious, trying to recover and heal from the damage and devastation the relationship caused. The true abuser will typically move on like nothing has happened. Commonly partying hard, quickly dating again and using the true victims' brokenness as proof that they are the unstable, crazy and the problem person they are claiming them to be. All too often, people buy into the narcissists' narrative and look on at the true victim and see their trauma symptoms as aligning to the abuser's narrative.

To perceive that there are two high conflict people in a messy and prolonged divorce is a misconception. The truth is the majority of high conflict divorces that drag out for years and cause absolute destruction along the way are typically a result of one high conflict person who is a narcissist or similar pathology. There are key elements that every high conflict divorce has in common. The abuser's need for control. The abusers need to win at all costs. The abusers need to seek revenge on their supply for leaving.

Losing control for this type of person results in a deep narcissistic injury to their fragile ego. This creates an obsession with regaining and maintaining control, dominance, and power over the person they were once in a relationship with. They will literally stop at nothing to destroy the person who has either finally left them, or who has showed signs of moving on. This often doesn't stop their incessant need to remain in control and all too often results in years of post-separation abuse. Many have claimed that leaving an abusive relationship, and it is definitely the case in my experience, that the post separation period is more traumatising and frightening than the relationship itself. What occurs in the post separation period when the narcissist realises they are losing control of their target is they will escalate to extreme levels, using any avenue they can to regain power and control. This often looks like strategic and horrendous smear campaigns to your family and friends with the motive to isolate you from your support network, if they haven't already achieved this during the relationship. It looks like vexatious litigation through the legal and court systems to keep you in a prolonged state of stress and drain you financially. It is often harassment, stalking, and trying to bait you into reactions that they have intentionally driven you to. There are commonly false allegations to police, child protection services or ongoing perjury or false claims within formal court documentation. It includes tactics to try to prove you are mentally unstable or crazy and this is commonly fraudulently falsified in documents and can be set up to bait you into reactions to use against you. They will use the very system intended to protect you to further control and abuse you.

If you have children, they will be used as pawns to inflict further fear and pain on you with complete disregard for how their behaviour is impacting their own children's lives. It is everything that allows them to maintain control over you and your life and prevents you from moving on to safety and freedom.

Unfortunately, the lack of accountability and consequences by the legal system for these behaviours can have an emboldening effect on abusers who use vexatious litigation, delay tactics and false allegations to cause further harm and stress. If there is no accountability for their behaviour within the system, then it proves to the perpetrator that their use of the system to control actually works, and they keep coming back to this source to feed their need for power and control over their victim.

The current culture of the court system often disregards this behaviour and enables this ongoing covert abuse, resulting in empowering perpetrators and causing further escalation and prolonged post-separation abuse. The legal system can unfortunately increase the risk to survivors in this type of dynamic rather than providing protection and justice. Although there are currently positive changes occurring in the family court system and talk of comprehensive reforms, it will be a long while before any significant change takes place to prevent perpetrators from using the system to further abuse.

Shortly after our follow up court hearing resulting in my ex-partner's false report on me being wiped, and his promise I would see a better man moving forward, his demeanour and behaviour shifted. I sensed it. I could feel it. I kept trying to seek confirmation from him he was going to follow through on our settlement agreements we had signed off on weeks before and that he was going to execute his required actions, as I had completed mine already. He affirmed everything was fine, and that he was just needing more time, because he'd been busy.

My anxiety escalated, and the more he could sense I was anxious with my personal power in his hands, the more he shifted the goalposts and gave me mixed messages as he stepped deeper and deeper into control. He somehow kept me holding onto just enough hope that he was still going to follow through in finalising our parenting and property settlement into legal orders, allowing me to finally be free and move forward in life and away from the stress and constant anguish. His demeanour was detached and there was an element of coldness and something unemotional about him, yet his words kept telling me he just needed more time and was committed to following through and finalising our agreement.

I knew something was off, but I couldn't put my finger on it. I wanted to focus on resolve for our children and Christmas was fast approaching, so I didn't want to create any more tension in our dynamic. I was not prepared to part with our children for their first Christmas day as a separated family and wanted to make the day normal for them with both parents present. My people pleasing trait was still rife, so the only way I felt I could manage the impending Christmas day was to ask my ex-partner to join us and spend Christmas morning in the home with the children and me. I thought if I had firm boundaries around it just being the morning part of the day and that he then had to leave, then it should be ok. The discomfort at the thought of him being in the same home as me was quite crippling. I didn't feel I had any other choice but to be fair to the children and to my ex-partner on this special day. I began putting measures in place for my safety and reached out to a friend to share with her my plan about my ex-partner being in the home for Christmas. She offered for me to use her as a way out at any stage in that I could state I was heading out to catch up with her if I needed to escape. She also communicated she would keep checking in on me while he was present in the home.

Christmas day approached and his anxiety inducing demeanour remained. I even confronted him on the day and said that we are due to put the family home on the market the following week as per our signed agreement and explained I sensed he may change his mind. He looked me square in the eye and told me I could trust him, that he was committed to following through on our agreement and reaffirmed that we would put the family home on the market the following week. I sensed in that moment that it wasn't genuine, but I disregarded it, as I was still in the pattern of believing his words and not listening to or even recognising my intuition.

On Christmas day, we did presents with the children and had a family breakfast. I was very shut down, and he was quite cold and we didn't really speak. He was only present with the children for about an hour when he disappeared somewhere in the home for a while. I left it and continued playing with our children, but became increasingly uncomfortable that he was roaming around the house somewhere. He had long moved out and taken his personal items, so there were really only my belongings left, aside from some joint furniture. I found him rummaging through my office and my drawers and files. He tried to cover it up by saying he was seeking something of his that he'd lost. I realised at that moment he was looking for something important. He had some bags of paperwork packed and items ready to take to the car. I didn't know what it was, but I was extremely concerned about how he was behaving.

Shortly after that, he said he was ducking off to the local café to collect a takeaway coffee and would be back shortly. He was gone for over two hours. I didn't understand it. He had insisted on spending Christmas morning with the children and now that he had access to our home, he spent his time sneaking things to take with him and then was not even present for the few short hours he had the opportunity to spend with our children.

He finally arrived back at the house and then said he was heading off to a Christmas day party with what I assume was his new girlfriend. I was dumbfounded. I began to piece it all together. He had not cared about spending Christmas with his children at all. He had been playing the game to ensure I allowed him access to the house, and Christmas day was the only opportunity I would allow for that to occur. Wherever he went for those two hours was not to get a coffee, as the café was less than five minutes up the road. It would later come to light exactly his motives for wanting access to the home on Christmas day. He had taken my personal files, my bank records, my journals and other personal items of mine. He was in the thick of a dark and calculated plan to trick me and eventually bully me into changing our property settlement to give him most of our assets that were predominantly the assets I had brought into the relationship when we met.

The confirmation he gave on Christmas day about selling the family home the following week was all a lie. The promise that he was following through on our settlement agreements to legal orders was all a stall tactic to get me off guard. The indication that he wanted to spend some time on Christmas day with our children was all aimed at gaining access to the home to take my personal items he needed to get a head start for legal proceedings. The manipulation was very well done. He knew how to work me. My world and the safety and freedom I thought was finally coming to me through the close out of our separation settlements and the arrangements for our children were all an illusion.

A calculated and pre-meditated plan was well underway to destroy me, my reputation, take all our assets for his own and to once again try to falsely incriminate me and taint my character as a mother to better himself in our parenting and ultimately financial outcome.

CHAPTER 13

THE DISCARD

A couple of days after Christmas, my ex-partner told me he wanted to meet for a chat about the plan for our upcoming house sale, and he came over and unexpectedly gave me a lengthy love letter. This letter was disturbing, considering we had been separated for over six months by this stage. It was a declaration of his love for me and stated his desire to work on healing our relationship and be a family again. It was full of apology, remorse and promise for change. It then casually led into his request that I sign the family home over to his name and that we don't sell, all disguised as his intentions being because he wanted to pay it off for our family and our future and to not burden me with the expense of its upkeep. It continued with intense requests and a detailed and obviously well thought out financial plan for my pre-marriage assets that he had insisted I sell. To add to this ludicrous attempt at love bombing and hoovering me into his trap, he continued by telling me he wanted us to go overseas and conduct gender selection IVF to have a baby girl together. He knew I had previously hoped for a daughter and he obviously thought this would be a way to manipulate me into his ingenuine plan for staying together.

Alarm bells were firing off with intensity while reading this love letter. My blinkers were off now. I had seen this cycle and could tell this was manipulation. He was trying to make me feel safe in our connection by wooing me with his words, false promises and future faking. All to have me drop my guard and give him almost all of our joint and my pre-marital assets. I knew he was dating other women and I could tell he was emotionally detached from me, so this letter was out of the blue and did not add up. I didn't entertain the love letter and reiterated firmly that we were still separating, that we already had our signed settlement contracts from our mediation and therefore needed to execute the agreement and plan. I left no room for there to be any other option aside from honouring our signed agreement to move forward and sell and finalise our settlement matters. What occurred in the moments that followed was the start of the most harrowing journey of survival I would ever experience in my lifetime. His mask would finally come off for good and I was about to experience the malicious and frightening discard.

Narcissists eventually discard people they claim to love when they have finally sucked and squashed every ounce of joy and self-worth from you. When they realise there is nothing left to gain from you, they cut you off completely like you are worthless. They will often escalate cold and callous treatment towards you if you still have ties with children or legal processes, but there will be no compassion, no respect and a vindictive and callous intent towards you forever more. It's black and white thinking. If you can't be their supply and they can't have you or control you, they will cut you off and focus on destroying you.

Realising his love letter had been unsuccessful in manipulating me to give the foundations he needed to execute his plan to walk away with almost our entire asset pool. His demeanour suddenly switched. He glared at me with the blackest eyes I have ever seen in my life on another human being. It was like he was possessed. It stopped me in my tracks. There was a void, a darkness and such intensity in his stare that if projection could kill, I would have been floored just by his intent. He went from zero to a hundred in the matter of seconds. He yelled at me, *"I have tried to be nice, but not anymore. You had better watch your back!"*.

He stormed off out of the house and left. It left me shaken and completely dumbfounded at what had just occurred. I still had the love letter in my hands and could clearly see his words written about how sorry he was and how he wanted to heal our relationship, be the husband I deserved, and to move forward. I realised as I stood there, that he had been a ticking time bomb these past couple of months but he had held together to execute his plan to manipulate me into thinking things were safe and moving in the right direction for closure of our settlement, and to keep me from voicing the truth in the follow up court hearing for his false report that had recently been withdrawn. I had a deep and terrifying inner knowing that things were about to get worse than I'd ever seen before. The panic set in. The months of chronic stress were already wreaking havoc on my physical and mental health, and now that I knew things were only just beginning, I was crippled with fear and fell into a deeply disempowered state.

He was due to have our children that weekend and he never showed up to collect them. The government had issued a fourteen day home lock down restriction for the COVID pandemic. I had no choice but to lock down with our children and was later to find out he had taken off to another town on a sailing trip and holiday with his new girlfriend, to escape the home lock down requirements and his parenting responsibilities during this time. He stopped contributing financially to the children's expenses that week also, despite us having a signed agreement in place.

Two weeks passed, and I reached out to him in a formal email to offer him a final opportunity to follow through on signing off our legal consent orders for our parenting and property settlement that he had already agreed to have finalised, but that he had failed to follow through on receipt of them. I advised him I was putting the house on the market the following week as per our signed agreement and sent him the evidence of our mediation outcome and his emails of him agreeing for us to follow through with securing it in legal orders. I continued with advising him I had moved forward with transferring my share of our savings as agreed in our signed agreement to my personal account. This last action had him flare up and attack. I realised this whole stalling process was about him trying to navigate how to financially benefit himself well above what his entitlement had been determined to be and to what we had signed off on to date. It was clear he didn't actually want to have our children regularly as it hindered his lifestyle, but he was fighting to have them so he could gain the financial benefit from more time with them.

When he finally made contact to have the children stay with him for his time, his demeanour was dark. He would stare down my car with such anger as I drove off from dropping the children to him, almost trying to intimidate me with his glare. It was unnerving. We had ongoing safety issues with the children in his care since we separated. Our twelve month old had fallen down the stairs twice in one week in his care and sustained a head injury, plus swallowed caustic dishwashing tablets while left unsupervised at his home which he hid and then failed to seek medical treatment for.

The children's car seats were frequently unattached and not secured in his car. He was regularly wreaking of alcohol at the handover of the children to him. It was awful as a mother having to hand over such young children to someone you knew was not competent or present enough to care for them at this age.

On one occasion when I dropped them off, and his demeanour was as dark as I had ever seen before, he snarkily made a comment about a dent in the door of my car. I hadn't actually seen this dent before, so assumed it must have occurred recently, but I didn't actually care. I had more important things to worry about than a dent in my car. I brushed it off and commented it must have been from a rogue shopping trolley. He wouldn't let up focus on this dent and stared me straight in the eye, then laughed evilly and told me that the dent wasn't from a trolley. It was very obvious he was indicating that he had damaged it and he wanted to make sure I knew. I just stared at him, realising what he had done and that he was trying to intimidate and scare me. I got in the car and drove off.

At home, I saw an email on my phone had just come through from him. It didn't make any sense. It stated that he was concerned about our children's safety in my care, claiming that when I dropped off the children just now, he had noticed their car seat was unattached in my car. The exact safety issue I had caught him out doing multiple times. I raced out to the car to check. Both children's seats were completely secure. The shocking realisation set in that he was trying to set me up and create evidence in writing against me to balance the factual safety events that had occurred with him. He had clearly tried to bait me into a big reaction about the intentional damage he did to my car, and I would discover later he was recording our interactions.

I feared he was plotting to go down the formal Family Court path, and he was trying to stall our settlement to have time to create and gain evidence against me to benefit himself in court. I was soon to learn that this is exactly what was going on and this was the exact plan he was calculating and plotting to execute.

CHAPTER 14

A Harrowing Survival

Sometimes the strength you are needing to find can only be accessed when you are driven by a purpose greater than your own needs. A purpose that shifts you from I can't do this anymore to an invincible force of I will never ever give up.

I realised this was psychological warfare. He had been playing a game of manipulation and deceit and a calculated plan to set himself up for entering the legal process since the day I left him. I also began reflecting on the now obvious pattern of behaviour that escalated slowly over the years we were together. Besides the slow and insidious psychological abuse amongst the betrayals and lies that were chronic and ongoing, there were also the more tangible and physical patterns of behaviour. First, punching a hole in the wall in my home. Then, strangling and choking me around my neck in the presence of our newborn baby. Finally, punching me in the face and knocking me unconscious. If I had stayed in this relationship, the next time could have been far worse. There had been no actual physical events since we separated, but the psychological tormenting was by far worse than anything I'd ever experienced with him now that he felt he was losing control of me. The most distressing aspect was that he went to extreme levels to cover up his history and paint me as the abusive one with anger management issues, using this narrative in false allegations to police and in court documents.

Later on, in his court affidavits and in his allegations in police interviews, he would repeatedly attempt to re-write history and twist the events to place him in the role of victim and me as perpetrator. It was one of the most frightening and disempowering experiences to be on the receiving end of. He was calculated and pre-meditated in his attempts to push me into reactions and intentionally try to re-traumatise me so I would react. There were many set ups and attempts to bait me into reactions which he secretly recorded, or where he would push me to absolute limits to cause me to write in emails, things that he would submit to court in parts and out of context. The tormenting and psychological abuse became so bad that I had to block him from my phone and messages. He would then pop up on my social media and continue to harass me and try to bait me into a reaction through that avenue. My reactions made him feel powerful and significant. He didn't care if it was negative attention he was getting from me, as long as he could feed off and take something from me energetically through my reactions to what he was putting me through.

The tormenting and intimidation continued to the point I had to block him from all means of communication to protect my mental health and sanity. This was not ideal and very challenging when trying to co-parent our children, but I did not feel I had any other

A Harrowing Survival

option at this stage. He had agreed to have our children stay with him every second weekend at this point in time. Despite this, he was very inconsistent and didn't show up reliably to have them. He would also often use the children as pawns to try further control and negatively impact me. This escalated even further once I went "no contact" with him. Shortly after, and on an occasion he had our children in his care, he failed to return them as per the time arrangement. I used to unblock one of the means of communication when the children were spending time with him as a channel for communication to discuss the children's care if need be. I contacted him to check in on where the children were and when he was planning on bringing them back. He ignored me. First for hours and then it progressed to overnight. I was beside myself. I was ranting and demanding in messages he bring them back. I realise now that this is exactly what he was after. He wanted me to feel powerless and under his control, giving him all my focus and attention. He eventually returned the children to me and acted as if nothing had happened and it was an innocent mistake. Not long after he left from dropping them home to me, I received an email from him through the unblocked email account. It casually stated that my fear about his sunglasses being cameras was not real and that I needn't worry. This was completely out of the blue and random. It didn't make any sense at all as we had never had any such conversation, so I just ignored it. I would learn at a later date that this was another attempt to gain written evidence for the plan he was executing to enter the legal process. I would later read in his court affidavit about this exact event regarding his glasses and the random email indicating I had asked if they were cameras. He wrote his affidavit painting me as an unstable and crazy woman, giving the example that I had once become paranoid while confronting him about a camera in his glasses that wasn't there. The specific and detailed scenarios he conjured up were disturbing.

Soon, I would experience a last straw moment with this man and the fear that he was intentionally trying to instil in me became too much. He finally responded to my email request for him to sign the parenting consent orders he had agreed to have drafted up for our settlement, and yet had failed to follow through on to date. On this afternoon, I received an email from a lawyer. It was a lawyer he had now engaged to begin legal proceedings, as I feared. The letter was horrendous. Aggressive. Intimidating. Down-right destabilising. This letter from his lawyer stated he wanted my financial disclosure to commence legal proceedings. It then continued on, accusing that I had run over his client's foot in an act of violence. Yes, that is right. He was stating in legal correspondence to intimidate me and to re-write history, that I had run over his foot in an act of intentional violence towards him. This was the same case that he had begged to have removed and wiped from the court, stating under oath that he had submitted this claim falsely against me as his wife in a moment of high emotion. The same event he had poured out remorse and apology to me to have my cooperation in remaining silent about this act of perjury. This same event he was now flipping the narrative on in formal legal correspondence without the slightest fear of consequences. I was beside myself. I remember I was due to collect our children from daycare at the time of reading the email and I wasn't able to for quite some time as I was hyperventilating and having a full-blown panic attack.

That evening and after I somehow put the children to bed in the state I was in, I call a domestic violence hotline. I was desperate for support and needed to know what to do. I requested to speak to someone who was experienced in coercive control. The counsellor on the phone was very helpful. She initially advised me to go to the police, but I explained that they had enabled him and been borderline corrupt in their involvement with his false

A Harrowing Survival

claim he had them initiate. She got it and understood what he was doing straight away. She actually really understood. Finally, someone could see what was going on. I felt validated for the first time. She was so concerned about my ex-partner's actions to date and the statistics on this exact pattern of behaviour leading to intimate partner homicide, that once she learnt he had moved only two hundred meters away from where I was living and that he was intentionally trying to manipulate the police, she insisted I come and stay with the children in a domestic violence shelter. This felt too big to even consider. I was still going to work at this stage, and I had our children to care for and to go into a shelter just seemed too extreme. When I said I could not do that, she insisted I consider submitting an application to the local court for a Domestic Violence Protection Order (DVO) on my ex-partner as a legally binding means of protection for me, both physically and psychologically. I realised through this woman who specialised in coercive control that my fears were, in fact, warranted. I already knew I was in danger, but I hadn't known what to do about it. I slept on the idea and decided to see how things progressed over the next few days.

After work the next day, I was out with the children. On arrival home that evening, I really needed some quiet time, so I put the children in front of a movie to entertain them while I went to lie down on my bed. I closed the door to the bedroom slightly to have a level of quiet. As I closed the door, I suddenly noticed that the doorknob was missing the locking latch I had used many times to lock the door. I stared at the space where the locking mechanism used to be. There was absolutely no way this locking mechanism could fall off or come out without unscrewing the whole door knob with a tool. I freaked out. I knew it was him. I knew he had removed this lock, but when? I had only recently locked this exact door a few days prior while showering in the ensuite when a contractor was at home. The door was still locked by the time the contractor had left and there was no one else who had visited since. My mind was racing. My nervous system was already completely stuck in an extreme state of hyper-vigilance. I didn't sleep a wink that night. I was already surviving on little sleep with the children still up multiple times every night, and the ongoing stress of the separation period to date. This added a whole other level of fear. I associated sleep with danger and developed quite severe insomnia. I was operating on empty. In fact, I was so depleted that I genuinely thought my physical health would not hold up much longer and felt the very real chance that my body may eventually malfunction in the way of a stroke or heart attack or that I'd develop a chronic illness from the prolonged and extreme stress causing so much inflammation on my system.

I continued on, trying to put one foot in front of the other each day and keep going. One night shortly after, I was closing the front door to our home at night when I saw a car's lights going slowly past the house, and then observed the car stop and idle up near the front of the neighbour's home. As I looked further, my heart dropped. It was my ex-partner's car. He was slowly driving past my home and had stopped just up the road slightly. I immediately flicked the light switch for the front porch lights to come on, and like clockwork, I saw his car speed off. He was watching the house at night. Now the lock had been removed. I couldn't take this anymore and knew I needed to do something. I sat up that night typing out my application for a Domestic Violence Protection Order (DVO), with the intent to stop him from being allowed to enter or come to my home and to prevent him from being able to contact me to intimidate me. I knew I had no other choice. I couldn't live like this. I had young children to care for and a job to maintain. I still didn't know why the lock to my bedroom door had been removed, but I knew for certain this man was out to destroy me and it was only a matter of time before he snapped completely.

My application was rough and messy. It was full of panic and written with such emotion. I was exhausted and had little time available when the children weren't around. I had to get it done quickly that night. I needed to get it in asap before another night went by. I wasn't sleeping. I needed some reprieve. For the first time as I typed out my concerns and evidenced events to date, once everything was put together in a timeline and sequential order showing the bigger picture, the realisation of what I had been in was shocking. I had the frightening realisation that this man may very well be capable of actually killing me. The chain of events and patterns of behaviour in our post separation period alone were horrendous. That coupled with traumatic events and toxic cycles that was our entire relationship. I knew I needed to do this for my sanity, to have space from his tormenting, to be regulated and calm for our young children. To allow some sort of space for my mind and body to seek a reprieve before it completely shut down from the stress that was being induced by him day in day out.

My attempts at boundaries were constantly disrespected and crossed. My request for space and limited contact was ignored and overrun. My ongoing attempts to resolve our settlement matters to diffuse the stress within the dynamic were intentionally being stalled. My desire for peace and some sort of rest was being intentionally disrupted daily. My nervous system would not hold up much longer. I knew I needed something in place to create a barrier from him to survive physically and psychologically. The more I asked for space, the more he infiltrated my world. I could also see that he was once again using false allegations through the legal system to scare me and try to destroy me that way. I knew that if I did not voice the truth about what the true history of his abuse and patterns of behaviour were, he was going to completely annihilate me with false allegations through the legal system, aimed at taking the children away from me for revenge. He had threatened this many times always as a means of control when he wasn't getting his own way.

Trying to achieve a level of safety through a DVO was a process I could never possibly have been ready for or aware of what lay ahead. The day I submitted my application, I unexpectedly received a phone call from a senior detective of the Vulnerable Person Unit (VPU) of the specialist police force. They advised they had intercepted my case in the system as they had flagged it at high risk. They explained my situation was textbook coercive control and high risk for intimate partner homicide with the strangulation assault that had occurred during the relationship. I was to learn that a history of a strangulation event is an evidenced precursor to a person being murdered by their partner in the early stages of leaving their relationship. I was further to learn that the first twelve months after leaving the relationship are most dangerous and the time a person is at most risk because of the impact the loss of control has on the perpetrator. It all made sense and was exactly how I had been feeling. It had felt too crazy to talk to anyone about my fears or mention any of these concerns. On the inside, however, I genuinely feared for my life from this man during this early post separation period, because of his demonstrated escalating behaviour and darkening demeanour.

The Vulnerable Persons Unit (VPU) insisted on sending a team to visit me at my home. I tried to decline as I was so shaken up by the experience and didn't want the drama, but they insisted and said it was the process once a case is flagged as high risk. They arrived at my home later that night while my children were in bed. They reviewed my documented evidence that backed up the claims in my application. The head detective told me she had seen enough to charge him right then and there with five charges if I wished to go ahead. One of these being the recent psychological abuse of the false police report he put on me, which came down to the criminal offense of perjury.

They explained that coercive control itself was not criminalised as yet, but advised it can still very much warrant a DVO to be allocated in civil law under domestic violence, to prevent further controlling and intimidating behaviour. This team of detectives advised me to push for criminal charges on my ex-partner, in addition to the protection order that they were confident would be allocated through the court. I had a lot of thinking to do.

My objective for this whole process was to seek physical safety and some reprieve from the psychological torture he was continuing to put me through, not to take him down in any way I could. Laying police charges was not something I had considered or wanted to do. I had to go away and think about my motives and what I was trying to achieve before making this decision. There was a part of me at some level still holding on to hope that he would stop all this controlling behaviour and change to have a desire and capacity to co-parent amicably for the children. I also knew that if I aggravated him through pressing charges, he would stall and hinder the completion of our property and parenting matters just to be difficult. I desperately wanted closure through achieving settlement to move on to freedom without this added element of chronic stress from our ongoing settlements remaining unfinalised.

One other concerning factor they informed me of was that if I handed over our children to him without legal court orders in place, he did not have to give them back and that there was nothing the police or anyone could do to retrieve them. They also shared the statistics of perpetrators in these circumstances who withhold the children, or even worse, harm them, to control the mother, and they urged me to get legal advice and consider my options for care arrangement for the children while our matter was without legal orders in place for our parenting arrangements.

I contacted my lawyer after this conversation and was advised immediately not to hand the children over to their father for any reason until our parenting arrangement was secured in legal orders. My lawyer then assisted me with drafting yet another set of orders and a final offer for my ex-partner to sign so he could begin having the children in his care. It was essential we established a legally binding order with relevant safety measures in place, and clear care arrangement before the children begun unsupervised time with their father.

The children remained in my care from this point, which I thought would only be a few weeks until we finalised our legal orders for parenting arrangements. There was no way that I wanted to or thought I was capable of, having these children 100% of the time 24/7 long term while trying to maintain my career, manage the consuming legal processes and be up most of the night with two young children still in nappies. I told myself I just had to manage it for a few weeks and that things would have to be sorted out soon.

The following week when the VPU reached out to ask if I wanted to proceed with criminal charges, I advised them that was not a path I was willing to take at this stage, as it would aggravate

A Harrowing Survival

him and explained I desperately wanted our settlement matters finalised. I continued on with the civil DVO process as that met my need of having a legal boundary between us and a deterrent for his escalating behaviour towards me. When my ex-partner received notification of my application, like clockwork, he contacted me through the co-parenting application and confidently asserted he was contacting me to let me know he had received notification of my application. I could tell that the way his message was written was to ensure I felt intimidated and to show me he wasn't affected by my pursual of this.

I attended court the following week and my ex-partner stood confidently next to his lawyer, who requested an adjournment. An adjournment was granted for one month. I was later to learn this is a common tactic and my ex-partner adopted this to stall the process and intentionally increase my legal fees to wear me down, drain finances and eventually push me into an outcome he wanted once I was crippled by the stress from the prolonged process.

A month later, at the next court date, my ex-partner stood boldly by his lawyer, seemingly unphased, and it was stated that he was contesting the DVO and requested the case go to a trial. The magistrate briefly reviewed both parties' affidavits and was convinced at this early stage that a Temporary Domestic Violence Protection Order (TDVO) was necessary to provide me a level of protection until the trial. A Temporary DVO was assigned to my ex-partner. A final outcome would then be determined on whether a Permanent DVO would be warranted.

Hearing that my ex-partner was contesting and requesting a trial rattled me to my core. I was terrified of the legal process and so intimidated by the authority of the courts, police, and lawyers. I was not cut out for this type of environment or level of conflict. He seemed so incredibly sure of himself. My lawyer reminded me it's just another intimidation tactic and assured me of the fact I had strong evidence. In the meantime, I had a Temporary DVO in place that prohibited my ex-partner coming within one hundred metres of me or my home and restricted his ability to communicate with me.

Despite this legally binding DVO in place, he began communicating with me through the co-parenting application that was purely intended for communication related to the children's direct needs. It was like he didn't even acknowledge the legally enforceable DVO stating he was not to contact me. He contacted me on this application with a very remorseful and somewhat heartfelt message. He indicated he was missing his children terribly and wanted to resolve our family law settlement promptly and requested I get rid of my lawyer and we do it amicably between the two of us without lawyers. Obviously, this raised alarm bells for me considering I had attempted extensively to drive a reasonable outcome since the day we separated and it had been met with nothing but manipulation, intimidation, stall tactics and failure to cooperate. He also had the consent orders in which he could sign off on to have regular time with his children. He continued with the communication and it became obvious he was trying to lure me into putting certain agreements in writing so he could use it as evidence somehow. I unnervingly sensed he wasn't genuine, although it was extremely confusing as his words were so real and I was so desperate to have finalisation and resolve so I wanted it so badly to be genuine.

After going around in circles for a while, I took charge and sent him an updated version of the parenting consent orders to sign if he was genuine. He failed to follow through on this and shortly after, I was bombarded with legal correspondence from his lawyer with intimidating and demanding requests. I was left shaken, frightened and betrayed once again and realised he hadn't been genuine at all. I didn't trust myself to know what was real anymore.

I tried to proceed with selling the home to push our settlement to a close, but my ex-partner refused to sign the papers to sell. He wanted to keep me stuck, unable to move forward and paying down our mortgage for him while I continued to live there. After another attempt to gain cooperation to sell and yet another refusal, I stopped contributing to the mortgage. My ex-partner attempted to intimidate me to continue payments, but I ceased and said I would stay until the bank repossessed the home. This seemed to give him the push he needed as the outcome of this would not serve him, so he finally signed the papers to sell the family home.

With the upcoming sale of the home I was living in with the children, I needed to work out and plan where I was going to live. I wasn't in a position to re-buy a home with our settlements unresolved and my ex-partner would not agree for the children and I to move into my pre-marital investment home, so I quickly needed to secure a housing option. We were in the middle of a rental crisis in our state after the impact of the COVID pandemic and there was next to no availability for rentals in our area. As I lay there that night worrying and overthinking about how to gain security and stability for the children and I, I had the realisation that I may be very well within my rights to move to another town. A town I had always wanted to live but had not been in circumstance that allowed this because of my career. My career was not a priority now, with the children having been in my full-time care for over eight months now, with my ex-partner failing to cooperate with finalising our parenting matter to spend time with the children. I had the idea to broaden my options for locations to live and not restrict myself to live in the same suburb as my ex-partner, like he insisted I must. I parked this idea, but it was in the back of my mind.

Selling the house was intense and required well over the capacity for what I had time or energy for. I conducted the entire preparation for sale with landscaping, repairs, cleaning before open homes and all the administration on my own while having the children in my full-time care and continuing working. My ex-partner refused to help or contribute to anything.

A month after the home had sold, and we were in the final weeks before the settlement day, as well as approaching our next court hearing for the DVO I had applied for that my ex-partner had chosen to contest to date, I headed to my local café one morning that I attended regularly. As I walked through the door, I stopped dead in my tracks. Sitting at the exact table I sit at almost daily waiting for my coffee to be made was my ex-partner. He looked up, and we just stared for a few moments before I asked him what he was doing there. He timidly began an out pour explaining that he was so sorry, expressing he had been a fool and had not treated me right. He went on saying that he missed his children and wanted to come to resolve now. It appeared so genuine and so real, and he even shed a few tears. I felt myself falling into it almost immediately. I quickly reset myself and told him I would send through an email with my conditions for agreement for us to convert to an updated set of consent orders to be signed to finalise our matter. I left the café and felt quite shaken yet an element of excitement that this really might be real this time and that we may soon have settlement resolve to allow for freedom and moving forward.

I emailed him that evening. He responded the next day saying he agreed with everything and said he would have his lawyer draft the documents this time to save me the time and costs. I allowed this to occur. What I received back from him in the way of the draft orders needed a complete overhaul, so I had my lawyer work on getting the documents to an acceptable standard. He had also included a condition that I remove the DVO in exchange for him signing our parenting and property settlement documents. He knew how desperate I was to achieve this and he had been stalling the process to date to torment and control me, in the hope I'd give up and walkway, leaving him with all the assets. This condition was not at all a part of our settlement agreement and should not have been a condition proposed by any means. It was blackmail at its finest. When I declined this, as I knew I needed protection in place, he acted casual, as if he accepted my decision and showed he still planned to finalise our settlement matters. As the days went by, he began to subtly change the goal posts and I experienced the onset of his typical bullying in phone calls. When I called him out on this, he'd quickly revert to being sweet as pie and apologising, while affirming he was genuine and wanted finalisation for the children. My head was spinning in confusion and my nervous system was only just holding on with the chronic and immense stress it had been enduring for so long now. I panicked. I felt so triggered and scared he wasn't going to follow through on the finalisation I so desperately needed. The more he sensed my fears, the more his behaviour escalated, and the more the mind games became like psychological torture.

He knew my deepest desire and greatest need since the day we separated was to have resolve of our parenting and property settlement so we could focus on co-parenting our children. He knew that this was the avenue to gain access to my heart and evoke the compassion within me to ultimately manipulate me for his own gain. Although he had given me no reason to ever trust him again and had literally abandoned his own children physically and financially for many months by this stage, I was so desperate to have our matter finalised, and the stress being so severe that I would have tried anything to get it done. He played on this need and executed his deeply deceitful, calculated, and manipulative plan. Even as I write about this event, I can feel the impact it had and still has on my nervous system in remembering how dark and evil this was.

One morning during this week of negotiating towards finalisation of our settlement as agreed, he called me with a sudden change of tone and demanded I formally remove the DVO or he would drag me through family court for years until I had nothing left and ended up homeless. This was his exact threat. My nervous system suddenly collapsed under the strain. My reaction was huge. I was screaming down the phone at him in absolute terror. My entire system was haywire and in complete overdrive, as if someone was literally trying to kill me right there and then. I couldn't believe he had strung me along all week pretending he was missing his children, apologising for how badly he had treated me and begging to finalise out parenting matters. He knew I had invested thousands in this week alone through my lawyer behind the scenes, fixing up the draft documents he provided. He had now completely flipped and was threatening me and literally blackmailing me to remove a very needed DVO, or he was going to drag me through court for years. As I screamed down the phone, calling him a psychopath, he calmly and eerily chuckled with an ever so calm laugh. It was like he was literally getting off on how much distress I was in and by how much he could impact me and bring me to my knees. In the calmest voice ever, he told me he had just recorded my outburst and would

A Harrowing Survival

share it with the police and the judge at our trial for the DVO, where he would contest this.

I was literally hysterical, screaming in terror down the phone. This whole façade was an attempt to manipulate me into signing off on removing the DVO, all while having me believe his motives were about him wanting to do what's right for his children in resolving our settlements. I had the sickening realisation he had never intended to sign off on our settlement matters to give me the freedom I needed or to spend time with his children. He was playing me the whole time in manipulating me into think he was going to have me apply to remove the DVO, and then he would have pulled out of our parenting settlement finalisation and not followed through. When he realised I wasn't going to remove the DVO application, he had just kept stringing me along knowing I was outlaying thousands to my lawyer along the way, toying with me, and plotting on how he was going to use the situation to his advantage.

This week was by far the most traumatic week of my entire life. The accumulation of severe and constant stress that had built up for so long now and yet another deep betrayal was too much for my system to cope with. I got off the phone and collapsed on the floor. I cried hysterically for hours, almost hyperventilating for most and eventually somewhat passed out in some sort of semi-conscious state. It was like I wasn't asleep, yet I wasn't awake or in my body. After what would have been a few hours, I picked myself up and called a counsellor and couldn't even string a sentence together. She understood what had occurred and said it was severe coercive control and a tactic to bait me into reaction and have power over me. She suggested I admit myself to hospital as I informed her I hadn't slept for what would be 4 nights straight that night approaching and hadn't been able to eat anything in days. I didn't even know it was possible to stay alive and literally not sleep for that long until this time. I told her I had to collect my children from daycare in a few hours and that admitting myself to hospital was not an option. That afternoon, I was still a complete mess. My jaw began to spasm and eventually locked up completely and I couldn't open or close my jaw at all. My body was in constant and involuntary tremors, and I felt like I wasn't even in or a part of my body anymore. I had not eaten a single bit of food for days, in addition to zero sleep. I literally thought I was going to die from my physical body shutting down. I had never experienced anything like this in my entire life.

Despite this, my children were not too far from my thoughts. I set my phone alarm for 5:45pm which is just before daycare closes for the night, and I took myself to the shower, turned the water on a lay there on the shower floor crying uncontrollably. When my alarm eventually went off, I was utterly exhausted and so incredibly weak. On autopilot, I picked myself up, still not able to speak or unlock my jaw, still trembling, and I got in the car. I put on a pair of sunglasses and drove around the corner to collect my children from daycare. On arriving home with them, they were their usual demanding and dependent selves, and I had nothing left to give. I gave them both a bottle of milk, took them to my bed, and lay there exhausted.

I still didn't sleep that night, so the next day I dropped the children to daycare early and took myself to the GP to request some Valium. I have never taken these types of medication in my life. In fact, I wouldn't normally even take a Panadol for a headache unless it was extreme. The GP took one look at me and gave me the script immediately. I took a dose and fell asleep for the rest of the day. Amongst all this, I was supposed to be at work and for the first time in my entire career of almost two decades, I had been a no show at work and hadn't even checked my work phone in a couple of days. I was in full-blown survival mode and work hadn't even crossed my mind. The following day, I ended up applying to take extended leave of absence. Little did I know, this was to be the end of this lifelong career path.

THE DEPTH OF HER SURVIVAL

ISOLATION — Sets out to destroy the entire support system of the healthy parent (e.g. friends, family, teachers, professionals & community) through manipulation, smear campaign, false allegations & playing the victim.

LEGAL ABUSE — Strategic stall tactics & false allegations throughout the legal process, wears a "mask" in the courtroom to fool even the most experienced legal professionals - behind the mask is calculated & malicious intent.

DISCARDING — Wages an ongoing war for unreasonable care arrangements for the children with underlying intent being control, revenge & financial gain. Once there is a "win" the children will often be discarded.

FINANCIAL ABUSE — Plays games to intentionally drain finances through vexatious litigation, commits contempt of court by failing to financially disclose as legally required, hides assets, unethical conduct in attempts to dodge financial responsibility to the children.

DV BY PROXY — Torments & further controls the healthy parent by using children as porns, compromises the healthy parents support system with calculated manipulation of all known avenues of support, bullying & intimidation through lawyers.

HARASSING & STALKING — Bombards healthy parent with intimidating legal correspondence, undertakes "tracking" of electrical devices, physical stalking, seeks information through mutual people, continually creates situations to attempt to "bait" the healthy parent into a reaction.

COUNTER-PARENTING — Holds onto immense anger towards the healthy parent & is solely focused on revenge & control, obsessed with "winning" at all costs & disregards the needs of the children in the process, refuses to cooperate with a reasonable parenting outcome & will often drag out legal proceedings without care for the impact on the children.

Post Separation Abuse Cycle

CHAPTER 15

INVISIBLE CHAINS AND FLYING MONKEYS

At the end of the day, the right people will fight for you. The right people not only care when your life is fun and easy, but when it is difficult and messy and you can't find your smile anymore.

He called that night to speak to the children on Skype. It was obvious he was not interested in talking to them but was trying to hurt me further. He knew how distressed I had been by his actions. He spoke to them in a happy, bubbly voice and told them he was on his way out for a nice dinner with some friends and then mentioned the name of one of my good friends' husbands, who was going as well. He was trying to make me feel powerless and, like he was completely unimpacted by what had just occurred and have me silenced in fear that everyone in my support network was on his side.

Over the following days, I ignored calls from a good friend whose husband my ex-partner had been catching up with and I couldn't bring myself to answer. I had sensed in previous interactions that she was being swayed by him by the comments she was making to me about how she felt sorry for him, as she believed he was just wanting to be a loving father. I knew this to be completely untrue. It was clear he had manipulated her into thinking this to take away my support. It was clear in the weeks that followed that he had no interest in having our children spend time with him and there was no urgency for him to finalise our parenting matters for their benefit. He was living the high life and enjoying not having to be a responsible parent or give up his lifestyle to care for children. It was all a façade and a big act of pretending he wanted to spend time with his children. He had had the opportunity right there to sign off on our parenting matter and begin spending time with them immediately, but he continued to stall to control me instead.

Our trial date for the DVO was fast approaching, and I was beside myself with anxiety. I knew what he was capable of. I had seen the false claims he had made in previous court documents and knew it would be no different this time. The evening before the trial day, his barrister contacted my legal representation and requested we come to a deal and not go to trial. He had had six months to request this. But he had dragged this out, contested it, demanded appeals, and now, after six months of stalling and acting as if he was invincible, he wants to accept the order without admission for two years instead of the typical five-year duration.

My lawyer advised me that besides it being a tactic to wear me down, it is likely because he would have been advised that if he goes through with the trial, the evidence is so strong that he would almost certainly be placed on a five-year order and it would be evidence on his record that can be used for criminal charges down the track. Accepting without admission meant that no evidence would be shown to the court and therefore no evidence kept on his record. My aim was to have the barrier in place for physical and psychological protection from him and with my mental state being so rattled at this stage, the idea of not having to be cross-examined at trial the next day and still achieve the protection I was seeking was appealing. However, I knew two years was not long enough. My ex-partner was likely to stall our family law settlement for two years to wait until his DVO had expired. My lawyer told me he had arranged a deal with the other barrister and explained that his reputation in the field was important so he told me I needed to accept as he needed to consider his reputation with other barristers in the local jurisdiction and wanted to come to an arrangement that was going to be beneficial to his colleague's client as well. I couldn't believe it. The lawyer who I was investing thousands in to represent me was openly admitting his priority was his own reputation amongst his learned colleagues, rather than my safety or future. I was beside myself. I felt so unsupported and backed into a corner with nowhere to turn. The stress was far too much for me to cope with already, and I knew I had no option but to just accept this. I accepted this, and they assigned my ex-partner a two-year DVO against him.

I was crippled with disempowerment after this event but knew I had bought myself some time to hopefully experience some reprieve from my ex-partner so I could start to recover and heal. My physical and mental health were completely destabilised. My lawyer assured me that our family law matters would be well and truly resolved within two years and then the threat and his focus on me would dwindle. I wasn't so sure, and I felt I was the only person in the world that truly knew the depth of who I was dealing with.

THE DEPTH OF HER SURVIVAL

Sure enough, over two years after this time today, our parenting matter remains unresolved as he continues to stall.

Just three weeks after the Permanent DVO was placed upon my ex-partner, my opportunity for reprieve was proven to be short-lived. My ex-partner had long cleared out his belongings from the family home and the only items remaining were what we had already signed off and agreed on for me to hold on to. Sure enough though, he changed his mind and decided he wanted access to a few more items from my allocation. His lawyer wrote to my lawyer requesting access to the house for a full weekend before we handed it over to the new owners. There was some back-and-forth correspondence with the outcome being that my ex-partner did not have consent to come to the home and that I would put aside a pile of extra things for him from a list he sent through. It was very clear he did not have consent and with the DVO in place legally restricting him from coming within one hundred meters of the home, so I wasn't too concerned.

On the weekend that followed, I was out for the day with the children. I had a friend who was helping me pack up the house advise me she had just left my home after she had been over there, assisting me with some tasks. Not long after she drove away from the home, my ex-partner called her on the phone asking if she was at my home to let him in. She was taken aback by this call and responded with no and ended the call. She didn't tell me until a few hours later and was apprehensive to tell me as it was clear he had been watching the house to see her leaving the property and she didn't want to scare me. I was a little shaken by this and it was unnerving, but I knew I was moving soon and wouldn't need to be there for much longer.

A few hours later, as I was having an early dinner at the park with our children, my phone rang. When I answered, I was met with an introduction from a senior constable at the local police station. He asked me if there had been any issues at my place of residence that day. In a somewhat shocked state, I responded with a no and asked him to explain why he was calling me to ask me this. He was quite short and rude to me in his communication, which was also odd. He continued on saying that my ex-partner had presented to the police station earlier to let them know I might contact them to report a breach of this DVO, but he had wanted to let the police know in advance that he had consent to come to the house. My ex-partner had committed a criminal offense in intentionally breaching a DVO. He has then shockingly had the courage to take himself to the police station to get in first with his narrative, in case I got home and realised he had broken into my home and breached his DVO. I couldn't believe what I was hearing. I couldn't believe he had the audacity and courage to intentionally commit a criminal offense and have such an inflated belief that he could manipulate the law by getting in first with his false narrative. This police officer had clearly bought into my ex-partner's narrative, as his tone toward me was harsh. My experience with this police station to date was nothing short of horrendous. There was not only complacency and downright incompetence, but it is becoming hard to deny the deliberate corruption from the very professionals who are supposed to protect. I don't think I'll ever truly re-establish my faith in the police or court systems for the rest of my living days.

This officer was obviously just covering himself by making a call with me to check in. I would later learn it was the same officer who had enabled my ex-partners false allegations months earlier, and he was still aligned to him and operating from ego in not being able to accept he had gotten our situation wrong.

This was the same officer who failed to conduct due diligence and even speak to or interview me before submitting such an incriminating report against me with not an ounce of evidence. I explained my ex-partner did not have consent, and that there was a DVO in a place in which he had intentionally breached. The officer advised he was already aware of that and told me to send my evidence to his email to back up this breach. It was an unbelievably hard situation to comprehend when I had grown up my entire life believing that the police are there to help people and can be trusted. I was shown insight into the dark web of corruption of many of those who were a part of these institutions and held positions of power that enabled abusers daily.

Trying to manage these intensely stressful events with the children in my full-time care was so incredibly hard. I needed space to process everything. I stayed away from the home that night as I was so shaken up by the fact he had broken in with complete disregard for legally binding restrictions allocated to him only weeks prior. It was later than night that I gathered my evidence and emailed it through. The evidence was strong, and I thought for sure my ex-partner would need to be held accountable this time. Surely he couldn't just get away with breaking into someone's home when there was written instruction that he did not have consent and had a DVO in place.

The following day I went back to the home. On entering, I felt sick at the thought of him breaking in. I got the shock of my life when I walked in. He had been through everything. He had raided my filing cabinet and taken all my personal files and the remaining records of my bank statements. He had taken the only bed I had left set up that the children and I had been sleeping in until we moved house. We now had nowhere to sleep. The most disturbing part was it was clear he had been through all the rubbish bins and had taken bank statements that I had thrown out and other personal documents I had disposed of. On top of this extreme invasion of privacy and unethical conduct, he had brought over empty boxes and a heap of rubbish and junk that he left scattered everywhere. There is no other explanation for this except he was trying to make more work for me in having the house ready for handover. It was a revolting act, and I was in horror at what had just unfolded. This man honestly believed he was invincible. That he was above the law.

I couldn't sleep that night and the next day I felt unwell and developed respiratory symptoms. I carried on and knew I had a huge week ahead with moving house and had no time for rest. My symptoms progressively became worse over the next few days. I had to have the house in tiptop shape for the handover inspection with the real estate. I was so unwell. During the nights, I was having to drag myself out of bed to attend to our children, who were still consistently waking up multiple times during the night. During the days, I needed to clear the entire house out and have everything completely removed. I could barely breathe and was extremely weak on the day before the house settlement and handover. I developed a severe pain in my chest and could only take a couple of small steps before having to sit and rest. I had never been this ill in my entire life. I knew something was seriously wrong. I would have given just about anything to have a full night's sleep and get some rest. This was not an option with the children in my full care and little support left, thanks to the impact of my ex-partner's smear campaign. I pushed on and was so stressed about not having the house ready for settlement day. At one stage, I had about twelve loads of boxes and large items to lug down the stairs, strap to the car, and drop to a friend's place just to get the house empty. The pain in my chest was so severe by this stage and my breathing became shallower. I felt like I was slowly suffocating. As I continued carrying loads down the stairs to the car, I was in so much pain and distress from my physical state that the only way I could keep going was to count out three steps, sit down on a stair to recover, and then try to regain my breath before taking another three steps.

I was sobbing, experiencing so much pain, weakness, and distress. So utterly exhausted. The lack of support I felt was crippling. There was no soft place to fall, and the weight of the world was on my shoulders. I felt so incredibly alone. Trying to regain my breath was all I could focus on. I'd work up another three steps before the same distress set in and rest was the only option. I did this for almost two hours straight until every single item from the house was on the front lawn. I was having to give every ounce of strength and resilience I had within me to keep going. I pushed on with multiple car trips back and forth, dropping off all the items to my friend's garage, who was not home. It was torture. My body was failing, but my mind told me I had no choice but to keep going. No-one else was going to do it. I had a couple of hours remaining before my children's daycare would close for the night, and I was experiencing excruciating pain in my chest by this stage. I was literally gasping for air. I knew I needed medical treatment. I also knew I couldn't go to hospital as they would admit me and I had no one I thought I could lean on to collect my children from daycare. I just needed a quick fix for now to get me through the night.

I took myself to a local medical centre that does emergency care. They tended to me immediately and made the diagnosis that I had well-established pneumonia. That made sense, considering my lungs felt as if they were collapsing. They connected me up to an Intravenous Drip (IV) drip and began administration of strong IV antibiotics. They placed me on high oxygen and administered some steroids for my lungs. They then began writing the notes and advised that they would call an ambulance to have me admitted to the hospital for further treatment. I just about jumped out of the bed. Between gasps for air, I told the doctor that getting admitted was not possible and that in less than an hour, I needed to be discharged to collect my children from daycare before it closed. He just looked at me in silence for a moment, almost to see if I was actually serious. He then said that the IV medication would take at least an hour until it was fully administered.

I panicked. I cried. I pleaded with him to make the IV drip run faster, as it was not an option to stay longer. He continued by saying I would need at least five days in the hospital for treatment and recovery. I was in such a state of overwhelm and had been so chronically distressed that all I could feel was panic. I began taking the tape off my IV drip as if to remove the IV canula out of my arm myself so I could leave to collect my children. He saw how distressed I was and told me he would be breaking medical protocol by fast tracking the treatment and discharging me, but that he couldn't force me to stay.

He sped up the IV drip, so it was completed before I had to leave. He then gave me a script for the highest strength antibiotics available to take orally. He also advised that it may not be effective and that I needed to work out a plan so I could present to the hospital in the coming days for further treatment. I thanked him and left to collect my children and headed home.

At home, we had no bed to sleep in, so we slept on the floor. It was a rough night, and I was still so unwell. My children didn't understand and were their usual demanding and dependent selves, which was challenging to tend to in my current state.

The next day, I drove to our new and temporary home in the next town that I had secured until I came up with a more permanent plan. I knew very well I was not in a fit state to drive, but once again felt I had no other option. I needed to provide a roof over our heads, and I just had to keep pushing through until we were moved in.

I was having to lean crouched to one side to take the pressure off the side of my chest that was still experiencing intense pain. My breathing was still weak and shallow, and my body desperately needed rest. I knew I just had to keep going for a few more days. To have the old home handed over acceptably, to move properly into the new rental and then all I had to do was look after the children and could leave any other non-critical tasks until I was well again.

I had almost arrived at the location of our new home when my chest pain became so severe that I had to pull over as I was fully crouched to one side just so I could breathe. I became too dizzy and lightheaded and knew I needed to get to a hospital. I had the children in the back of the car, so was trying to remain calm on the outside to not scare them. I searched on my GPS via my phone for the nearest medical centre and when I regathered myself, I headed straight there. Stopping to rest on the side of the road when I needed to. I finally arrived and could not carry my youngest child because of the pain. He was screaming and crying for me to pick him up and carry him, but for the first time, I wasn't capable of doing so. I tried and tried, but the pain was so severe I kept dropping him out of my arms. I literally had to drag him by his arm, screaming into the medical centre. It was so distressing and such an awful experience as a mother to have the only option being to drag your distressed and screaming child along the ground.

I was tended to straight away, and they conducted a chest x-ray. It was determined that I had severe pleurisy, which is inflammation and fluid in the surrounding lung wall cavity, and the untreated pneumonia had caused scarring on my lungs. They advised me I needed to be admitted to the hospital. Once again, I had to decline. It wasn't an option and there was no one who I thought I could call on to have my children for overnights. The extreme and prolonged trauma I was experiencing had my rational brain highjacked and feeling nothing but constant terror. I truly believed there was no one I call on or rely on as everyone in my life at that stage was under the spell of my ex partners' manipulation. I felt I had no one I could trust.

The following day, I was miraculously blessed with a call from a friend who hadn't turned her back on me, but who was experiencing her own life challenges, so I had felt I wasn't able to call on her in this way. She offered to have my children for a couple of days so I could have medical treatment to get back on track with my health. It was a godsend. I don't know what would have happened if this friend hadn't reached out with such a generous offer. It was what I so desperately needed.

Reflecting on this period, the lack of support I felt, the feeling that I couldn't call on anyone for help, even in my darkest times, I can see how this was driven by the fear and almost paranoia my ex-partner intentionally tried to create through his smear campaign to my support network. I felt so deeply insecure about what my own friends thought of me because of what he had been saying. I felt so much shame about what was going on and that I didn't know who was believing him and who was still a genuine and loyal friend. I shut down, too fearful to reach out to my own friends in case they were judging me, believing my ex-partner and possibly not even a friend at all anymore. I didn't know who I could trust or rely on. It was the loneliest place in the world to be, and all strategically crafted by my ex-partner to ensure it became exactly that. To back up my fears, I received a phone call from my then so called best friend. It was a horrendous call. She didn't know how unwell I was but she began attacking me the minute I answered the phone, telling me how selfish I was for moving the children away from their father, telling me I was only thinking of myself and that I wasn't putting my children's needs first. She was completely convinced that I was withholding the children from their father for no reason other than spite and told me I needed to let go of him and move on. I couldn't believe it. He had actually convinced her I was the one not letting go and that he was a loving father who desperately wanted to be spending time with his children. I was so overwhelmed. I desperately tried to explain the truth of what was happening and justify everything, and she just kept cutting me off. She wasn't the slightest bit interested in hearing my side. She was convinced my ex-partner was innocent.

Her husband was a big drinker and he and my ex-partner used to drink together, so I almost feel like she just took sides with him to align with her husband. I was absolutely distraught. This was the one friend who I had always seen like a sister and she had now completely turned her back on me and sided with someone who was abusing me behind the scenes. This was the same friend who had been told about the physical assaults during the relationship. However, her mind was made up. The last thing I needed amongst a crisis and when I felt like I was almost on my deathbed in relation to my physical health, was my so called friends calling me and attacking me about my own life choices and decisions as a mother. I knew with every ounce of my being that everything I was doing, including leaving this toxic marriage, was for my children. I was doing it all for them and this was so hurtful to experience and immensely disempowering to be chronically misunderstood by those who were supposed to care for and support me. This was another blow and another layer of trauma to carry.

My ex-partner was by far winning this game of setting out to destroy me. It was working. I felt every aspect of my life was being destroyed by this man. Unfortunately, this friend was a leader and almost the matriarch of a larger group of friends I was a part of, and her opinion tainted and influenced the rest of the group. They slowly faded away and although I still hear from some of them occasionally, it feels as though they are just reaching out to get the gossip of my situation, so I choose not to engage. I have let these people go. It was hard, especially at a time I needed support the most. I realised however, that holding onto people who don't value me for who I am and who don't exhibit the core values that are important to me in a friendship, was just holding onto them because they were familiar yet not necessarily healthy or good for me. Anyone who knows your story yet invalidates your experience and sides with your abuser is toxic themselves. It is incredibly scary to let go of what is comfortable and familiar, even if it's not healthy for us. This was another of my biggest learning and life lessons that came out of this situation. I learnt the hard way to respect and value myself enough and have the courage to release with grace and ease those people who don't treat me with love and respect and those who don't see me or accept me for who I truly am. As an act of self-respect and self-preservation, I have chosen to have no contact with anyone who knows my story yet is still supportive of or associates with my ex-partner.

When we have spent our whole life feeling like we don't belong and experiencing the absence of a secure attachment to a caregiver, the innate coping mechanism is to be who others expect us to be. We naturally gravitate to be and play the role others place us in, to keep the connection and sense of safety in the dynamic. As we begin to heal and transform into a more authentic version of ourselves and adopt a higher level of self-esteem, any unhealthy connections will likely fall away. These dynamics will probably develop tension as you shift further away from the person they always knew you to be and the person they expect you to remain as. There is a misconception in our society and culture that friendships should last forever and that if they don't, then someone is wrong. Friendships can run their course for lots of reasons and although some friendships can become toxic, it doesn't always mean someone was a bad friend. Sometimes we evolve, our values and priorities may change, and certain friendships are simply no longer healthy or beneficial. Releasing the fear-based pattern of the need to hold on to what is familiar instead of what is healthy and good for us is linked to every aspect of a survivor's life, including friendships.

When you begin to live in alignment with your values and stand firm in your beliefs, you will drift from those who only accepted the version of you that prioritised fitting in with their ideals, limiting beliefs, conditioning, and the role they have always expected you to hold.

CHAPTER 16

WILL I EVER BE FREE

Here I was living in a new town, in a tiny rental unit with my two children and two dogs. Having recently resigned from my long-term career and solely focused on surviving every day as I independently cared for and parented our children. All while trying to deal with the onslaught that was the legal process of family court. It was more than a full-time job practically and even more so energetically. I was well over capacity for what was comfortable or possible to sustain. The physical distance from my ex-partner helped me to feel physically safe, but he ramped up the psychological abuse now that I had gotten away.

He hadn't spent time with his children for what was approaching a year by this stage. He barely spoke to them on Skype regularly anymore and it was like his children were discarded and the furthest from his mind. He kept the intensity of the legal proceedings going with games, stall tactics, ongoing intimidation and bullying that had me gasping for breath most days, trying to keep my nervous system stable. Amongst all this, the police officer who had reviewed the evidence for his breach of his DVO and the break in, ended up being ever so complacent and basically did nothing. I knew I had to take a stand to put a stop to this escalating behaviour from him once and for all. I made a complaint up the ranks in the local police station to the senior management regarding this severe breach of my protection. In particular, the lack of action taken by the police who had been enabling him from the start of his interactions with them.

My case was transferred to another police officer and through the investigation that finally occurred, my ex-partner was suddenly charged, arrested and locked up in the police watch house that same day. The investigation showed that it was in fact a severe and intentional breach, and he was given a court date for a sentencing. Leading up to his court date, his legal representation attempted twice to apply to have the charges dropped. The investigating officer rejected this request because of the strong evidence. Unfortunately, this officer went on extended leave a few days before my ex-partner's sentence date in court and was not accessible on the court date to support the case. I wasn't required to attend his court days, but the evening of the day he had been sentenced, he rang the children on Skype in a familiar bubbling and almost buzzing tone. I knew instantly he had gotten away with this breach in court. I could tell by his demeanour on the call with the children. Sure enough, the next day I was informed that he manipulated his way in court to receive a slap on the wrist and no consequences for breaching his DVO, which is an actual criminal offense. He had pleaded guilty to avoid a trial, and because of the accountability and remorse acted out that successfully manipulated the magistrate, he was only given an informal warning. Once again, no consequences, and he clearly felt invincible.

I was feeling so helpless and disempowered. It was like he really was above the law. The system was so flawed that it was actually placing me at more risk instead of protecting. Every time he got away with such things, his behaviour would escalate. He felt invincible and would come after me harder and with more intensity than ever before.

I tried to desperately push for our settlements to be finalised again. I needed to escape this dynamic. I needed it to end. He just wouldn't let up or cooperate, no matter what I offered. I cried myself to sleep most nights for such a long time, feeling utterly hopeless and in despair that he was never going to ever let me be free.

I was banished in invisible chains that only I could see and feel. I realised with his increasing absence towards our children that the reason he wasn't cooperating with finalisation, aside from the control aspect, was that he didn't actually even want to have his children. Once he actually signed off on legal orders, he would have to have them every second weekend. His lifestyle at present did not allow for this and he didn't have any motivation or drive to finalise our matter. He was off on weekend sailing trips, overseas and interstate holidays regularly, out for dinner and drinks multiple times a week, and the list goes on. He was using me having the children full-time, saying I was withholding them so he could play victim to everyone around, while happily not having to uphold his parenting responsibilities.

He had every opportunity to have the children every second weekend since the day we separated, but he chose not to finalise and therefore not see them at all. Once again, image management was everything. He would never admit to others that he didn't want his children, so he instead manipulatively played the narrative that he had no choice and I was withholding them.

I recently dangled a giant carrot in front of him to encourage him to follow through on finalisation and offered to remove all financial obligations or contribution to his own children for the rest of their childhood, including formally voiding his mandatory child support responsibilities. Sure enough, this did in fact lure him to move toward the resolve of our parenting matters after all this time. It was so clearly all financially driven and has been the entire time. When I think about this, it terrifies me to think of our children transitioning into his care now long term, knowing that he has never put their needs first and has never once acted in their best interests during our entire separation.

It is a fear I am working on every day to eventually be at ease and find peace with the journey my children will embark on with their father when the time finally does come for them to be in his care again. Until then, I rest in peace for the time being knowing they are happy and thriving at present and that they have developed a level of resilience that will carry them through the likely dark and confusing times that lay ahead with their father's behaviour.

Our divorce has immensely impacted our eldest child and, in particular, his father's absence and inconsistency. When he was three and a half years old, I saw a shift in his normal assertive and outgoing personality. He became withdrawn, anxious, and focused on appeasing and pleasing others. I recognised this as his fear of rejection and abandonment playing out. In the year after we first separated, his kindergarten was planning father's day activities. They invited all the dads to come to kindy for an evening fire and concert. They were planning it and practicing at kindergarten leading up to this. Our eldest withdrew at home and I could sense it deeply troubled him, but he was suppressing whatever was going on for him. He ended up breaking down in tears and sharing that he thought his dad was going to miss out on father's day at kindy. He hadn't seen his dad in many months by this stage. I had already reached out in legal correspondence to request he finalise our matter in time for father's day and provided details of the kindergarten event.

I felt immense grief as father's day drew closer and I received no reply, not a single mention or acknowledgement from their father about my attempts to organise for the children to see their dad on this day. I went to the level of demanding in legal correspondence that he at least book a visit with the children for father's day itself. It was met with silence.

I was later to discover he had gone away on a weekend sailing trip instead of seeing his children on father's day weekend. I kept our eldest home from kindy on the day the father's day activities were on at kindergarten in the week prior, as it was the only way I could think of to somewhat protect him. On the actual father's day weekend, I didn't mention to the children it was father's day and instead took them out for a special breakfast, yet treated it as a normal day. It was a heavy day for me. I was full of grief for my children and feeling so heavy and powerless in not being able to fix this for them or make it better to protect them from this pain. That night, our eldest pulled out the father's day gifts he had made his dad at kindy and began showing me through them as he had been doing every night for weeks. There were some chocolates in there that he insisted he needed to save for his dad to give to him on father's day.

The strangest and most profound thing occurred that night, which was the actual father's day night. We all went to sleep in the same room and our eldest child, woke up the next morning, sat bolt upright and asked ever so calmly, *"was it father's day yesterday?"*

I was shocked. He would have not understood what day it was or when father's day actually was. He then continued on to tell me he had a dream in his sleep and he had seen his dad and given him his father's day gift. He then quickly crawled out of bed to check his cupboard for the father's day gift he had been holding out to give him. His face dropped as he saw it was still there and this dream he had was just that, a dream. I could tell he was feeling hurt, but he was suppressing and pretending he was fine. He then took out the chocolates from the father's day gift bag he had been keeping safe and looked at me with a cheeky grin, saying, *"maybe we can eat these now because daddy is taking too long."*

We sat there on the floor eating the chocolates and it was like a wave of acceptance washed over him and he had the closure he needed to move forward through his dream.

My ex-partner didn't see or attempt to stay connected to his children for almost a year. It wasn't until our family court date for property settlement approached that he suddenly began acting as if he wanted to have visits with them after what was approaching a year of not seeing them at all. It was all to do with him trying to establish some sort of time with the children to increase his entitlement to the property pool. It was revolting to witness this play out. It was like he was trying to strategically use his children for selfish gain to tick a box and now show he was involved with them.

He could not fully commit to seeing them regularly though and was in obvious conflict with his priorities and his lifestyle. His other interests came in first every time. Once he came back into the children's life and opened them up to connecting with him again through these initial visits, they became somewhat attached to continue seeing him. I literally had to force him through legal letters and try to ensure he had no option but to turn up and visit his children as I was trying hard to protect them from the rejection and abandonment his inconsistency was causing.

I insisted he commit to visiting every second weekend, until our parenting matters were resolved. It had become mission impossible to get him to actually show up or be reliable and he had only recently re-entered the children's lives. He finally agreed to book a series of fortnightly visits to see the children. It was confirmed in formal correspondence and agreed in writing by both of us and the supervised contact centre where the visits were to be held.

The first two visits proceeded. On the third visit, I turned up to drop the children off and was advised he wasn't there and they couldn't get hold of him. As it was all new to the children, I could make a light-hearted situation out of it and say we must have got the day wrong and we'd come back next time. I then took them to see a friend they love playing with and they were happily distracted from what had just occurred.

I made a point of calling out this no show and the impact it had on the children to my ex-partner and thought that would be enough for him to pick up his game. A fortnight later, I took the children to the centre for the next scheduled visit he had arranged. Only in the lead up to this, I made a big deal to the children about them seeing their dad to compensate for the previous disappointment. Our eldest son was so excited and insisted we drive around town looking for superhero cookies to give to his dad. We spent the morning doing exactly that. I could sense our eldest was suppressing some anxiety leading up to this visit, and this was confirmed when he had a complete meltdown after he dropped and broke a cookie. He was distraught that the cookie wasn't perfect for his dad. It was heartbreaking. I could see at his young age he already felt he needed to perform and earn his father's love, acceptance and approval.

To top off his already fragile state in relation to his dad, after dropping the children off to the centre for the visit, the coordinator came running out to my car before I drove off to advise me that their dad had not showed up yet. My heart sank. She tried to call my ex-partner multiple times. No answer. I knew how much this was going to disappoint, hurt and fracture the children. They had opened themselves up to their dad again after a long period of healing and accepting he wasn't around anymore, and then he abandons them all over again so suddenly. I walked into the centre and saw my eldest sitting there in anticipation, carefully cradling the broken superhero cookie in his hands. He looked up at me and did not know the news I was about to break to him. I was almost in tears before even telling him. I carefully and softly shared with him and his little brother that daddy must be stuck in traffic and cannot make the visit today. As I watched in anticipation, hoping it was landing softly on them, our eldest stared into space and his face dropped. He was holding back tears. I could tell his little mind was racing, trying to work it out.

He broke down in tears as I carried him to the car. He then began kicking the back of the seat of the car in anger before going silent and staring out the window as I drove off. As I checked on him in the mirror, he looked as if he was in some sort of trance and was rocking in his car seat and quietly whispering on repeat while staring into space saying *"It's not true. It's not true"*. I couldn't hold back my tears and the pain and grief I felt for his little heart was immense. He is such a sensitive and intuitive soul, and I knew he knew his dad had not shown up for him that day. I knew he was internalising it as if he was unlovable and as if there was something wrong with him to make his dad not love or value him enough.

When we arrived home, I took him to a neighbour's house for him to have a distraction and do some building outside with the husband. It was just what he needed. On arrival home he appeared okay on the surface but was very clingy towards me and at one stage said out of the blue, *"mummy, your heart is connected to my heart because if I'm sad it makes you sad."*

He was referring to the tears I could not hide when observing the pain and confusion he was experiencing hours earlier. In the weeks that followed, he sunk into a dark place. I could tell he was depressed. He didn't have the motivation or energy for anything and began crying and clinging to me at drop off to kindergarten every day.

My ex partner had acted like he wanted to have the children more frequently, yet he couldn't even keep up consistency for over two occasions. He had caused incredible damage to the sense of self and self-worth of our precious boy. He opened the door to their fragile hearts and played with them for nothing more than his own selfish gain. This was similar behaviour that I experienced in our relationship and he was already portraying the same treatment towards his own children.

We approached the court date for our property settlement. The bullying from his legal team, under obvious instruction from my ex-partner, became so severe that the anxiety it induced impacted general functioning of my everyday life. All I could do was hold on for dear life and try to breathe through each day. I took the children for outings on weekends and socialised with others on occasions, but I was always pretending I was fine when it couldn't have been further from the truth.

I lived with a constant constriction in my chest, my breathing was always heavy, my heart was racing constantly, and I was hypervigilant to every sound and change in expression from others, or anything at all. I felt severely and chronically unsafe in my body and in this world. Looking back now, I don't know why I always allowed my personal power to be sucked dry by this man's bullying. He knew exactly how to play on my vulnerabilities and fears and bring me to my knees. Protecting my energy, taking back my personal power and not allowing this man to infiltrate my world and destabilise me, was a long way off at this stage and the hardest aspect of my healing I have had to work on mastering.

To make matters worse, I was fast running out of my savings that I was living off and funding my legal fees with. Because of the requirement for financial disclosure to which I complied with in full and cooperated with any request they sought, he could easily work out my finances were in dire straits and I'd be out of funds to live off soon. This resulted in him executing extreme stall and delay tactics and last-minute requests to have adjournments and push dates back to push me into financial ruin and stress so I would be easier to manipulate. It was clearly an intentional tactic to drain me completely dry of finances, so I had no option but to give in to everything he wanted when the final mediation came before the court trial. He failed to cooperate with his financial disclosure repeatedly and was hiding and moving assets overseas through a family members' offshore connections. Despite the requests for compliance to this mandatory court requirement for mutual full and frank disclosure, after eighteen months of trying to gain compliance from him, he still failed to do so. He was repeatedly in contempt of court without a single fear of consequences.

On our last and final attempt at mediation prior to our trial, I had completely run out of funds, I had tens of thousands owing to my lawyer that I couldn't pay until we reached a property settlement so I couldn't afford to continue in the court process. My ex-partner's parents had been funding his legal fees the entire time, so he was unimpacted by the financial strain that court proceedings cause. He could also maintain his high paying job as he didn't have limitations in caring for our children, so had all the time in the world to focus on his career. The impact of the stress was so severe during this period and I was desperate for things to end. I ended up being pushed into an unjust outcome just to have it done with, as I knew I couldn't cope with being in this state for much longer. He would not have budged and would have dragged it out as long as he could. He knew every tactic in the book for stalling, creating immense pressure, manipulating the court system, and incredible courage in committing contempt of court while displaying next to no fear response to this illegal conduct. I was fighting a battle with someone who did not have a conscience and believed they were above the law.

I realised I didn't stand a chance. I had done everything by the book. I could hold my head high knowing I acted with integrity and cooperated with everything required of me. Did this benefit me in this process? Not in the slightest. In fact, my honesty and compliance were a severe disadvantage. Was my ex-partner held accountable for his contempt of court, perjury, and vexatious litigation? Not even slightly. I certainly didn't win the war on the material or the practical side for acting with integrity, but I believe if there is such a thing as karma or life after death, then this man is going to be in for a very rough ride. To live life intentionally trying to destroy another human being and your own children is not something that, at a soul level, we as humans get away with. It's not about wishing harm or holding onto bitterness towards those who harm us, it's about providing yourself the validation you need to know that staying true to your values and being a good human, despite the outcomes along way, is what is going to give you inner peace at a deep soul level in the long run.

CHAPTER 17

Riding the Waves

I felt a wave of relief that the process was over, but I also had an immense feeling of anger and an overwhelming disempowerment that consumed me for quite some time. Why did I continue to give my power away to this man? It was like he still had full control over me energetically and I continued to slip into the dark hole of fear and powerlessness in the situation. I realised I had not consciously felt anger through this entire process. I had experienced terror and fear, but anger felt foreign and was not an emotion that had been felt, expressed or processed to date. It was definitely there and I could feel the intensity of the surge that was being suppressed inside me. I knew this wasn't healthy, and I sought techniques and strategies to express and ultimately process this anger. I came to the acceptance that I had every reason to be angry, but also had the belief that anger only hurts ourselves. My internal anger did not affect my ex-partner. It affected my health, wellbeing and happiness.

I was raised to believe I was bad or naughty, showing anger. It was always shamed, shut down and controlled into suppression. I still struggle with emotional suppression to this day from this form of unhealthy conditioning. I am very aware of this and it is something I continue to focus on and work through in my personal healing. Anger is simply an energetic charge. It is not good or bad, it is just an emotion in the same way we feel joy, sadness or anything else. It is expressing that anger in a safe and healthy way that is the key.

Learning to accept all of our emotional experiences takes practice and conscious effort, but it is one of the most valuable parts of our personal healing. Suppression of difficult emotions wreaks havoc on our health, the nervous system, and every aspect of our being. It is the suppression of these difficult emotions that results in the eventual unhealthy expression of such emotions that have been bottled up for so long. Or we disconnect from ourselves and our body and live in a state that never truly experiences life to the full, or deep connections with others.

Life continued to be experienced as an enormous struggle. I tried my best to focus on what I could do to support the children in getting involved in the community and developing connections with people to have in their life. They were happy enough, but the chronic and immense stress I was under took its toll on everyone. I didn't have capacity with the barrage of legal proceedings hitting me constantly, to always be present and calm. I gave them everything I could, and I also had to prioritise legal proceedings or he would take me down. This experience robbed them of their early childhood years to a certain degree, but I was so conscious of their needs and the potential impact that I did what I could within the capacity I had at each moment along the way. I still carry guilt and grief for what they have been through, and I have also learnt to adopt self-compassion for knowing I did my very best amongst the horrid circumstances.

Our children have had lessons, experience and adopted a level of capability and resilience that others their age haven't had the need to. This experience will shape their life and adulthood. There will be lifelong healing for them to work on through their own personal journey if they choose, and there will also be invaluable lessons and gifts that they will take with them into their future lives from their adversity. I know one thing for sure, is that no matter what, I will always be here for them through whatever presents for them in whatever way that is and as hard as it may be.

Shortly after our property settlement was finalised, he suddenly escalated and began hounding me about our parenting matters. It was like he needed to feed off my fear and wanted to keep the pressure and impact on my life going. I had constantly pushed and driven for resolve of our parenting matter since the day we separated and he literally had shown little to no genuine interest in being a decent and reliable father to our children or cooperating with any kind of resolution. Now that he was on a roll in having power over me and winning with our settlement outcome while causing maximum adverse impact on me along the way, he was coming in for the kill to disrupt the most important thing in my world. Our children.

"I know you thought breaking was the most painful chapter. It wasn't. Turn the page. The next part is much longer. It's the healing. The rise. The comeback. It's the birth of the new you. And it's not easy. But you are strong and brave and worth it." Stephanie Bennett-Henry.

CHAPTER 18

Phoenix Rising

For those who have left or are considering leaving a relationship with this type of person, it's so important to understand how they operate to prepare yourself and avoid being sucked into the spiral of chronic fear. There needs to be a focus on anticipating their next move, but rather than from a fear based and all consumed place, it is about planning how to work around the strategic tactics at play and put yourself in the best position to mitigate the effects of this.

What I saw clearly through my separation and what I have witnessed in my work in supporting others attempting to leave a similar dynamic, is that first they will nearly always go after money. They will be hardcore and relentless in trying to take everything they can from you foremost. Once they can no longer control you financially and there is little left to gain from finances, they will go after what matters most to you…your children.

They know your children are the most important thing in your world and they will go after what is closest to your heart. The children are too often used as pawns to further control and hurt you. Plan for this to occur. Be prepared and conduct yourself in a way where there is nothing for them to use against you at a later date if you end up in family court. Seek the support you need from professionals and make your recovery and healing a priority over anything. You can't care for your children, stand up against this level of evil or survive a broken court system if you are a dysregulated, reactive mess and can barely function. Put yourself first and seek support the entire way. Your future self and your children, if you have them, will thank you for it.

The intensity of my ex-partner around his newfound desire to resolve of parenting matter came in bursts and cycles. We attended two more parenting mediation sessions. The impact the mediation days had on me was destabilising and took me days to recover from. When we would get to the point of yet another agreement to finalise, he would play games, stall and fail to follow through in the weeks that followed. This occurred repeatedly until I finally reached a pivotal transformation point in my healing. Not without a few more breakdowns along the way, but I finally got there. I reached the acceptance that he was possibly never going to follow through on finalising our parenting matter. We had now had three mediation attempts that had resulted in three agreements that he failed to follow through on every time. I had spent almost three years straight consumed with trying to seek cooperation from him for finalisation of our parenting matter.

I knew something had to change. I knew I couldn't keep living like this. Always in fear, life on constant hold, waiting for the next unpredictable move from him. I had a belief that I needed him to give me closure before I could move on and experience freedom and inner safety. I thought I had to keep driving the process and doing everything in my power to encourage him to finalise our parenting matter so I could finally be free. I also believed it was in the best interest of the children to be spending some sort of time with their father and knew I couldn't pretend to them and cover for him forever. I realised after our third parenting mediation that resulted in an agreement that was reneged on yet again that getting closure from him may never happen. I had the realisation that I needed to give myself closure. I needed to take action that was within my control and take back my personal power in the dynamic. Of course I had tried to do this all along, but with the impact that the resulting trauma had created and the associated nervous system dysregulation that I was living with as a result, it wasn't something I had had capacity to achieve as yet.

The time came when I finally had a surge in my transformation and developed the strength and ability to stand firm in my power and take back control of my life. I had been trying to do this but had not had the capacity to truly align with this and shift the deep routed limiting beliefs and programming to the level I needed to. I could finally stand up for myself without living in fear of what he would do to me or the disempowering belief that the corrupt court system would annihilate me.

There was also an element of me having learnt from my ex-partner over time it was possible to get away with just about anything in the court system if you were clever and strategic enough. There were little to no consequences for things that really should have people held to account. The success within the court system ultimately came down to who could and was prepared to lie and manipulate skilfully in court, and who had the most money to throw at the most experienced lawyers. It had very little to do with justice or what was in the best interest of the children. I had been so fearful of the authority of the legal system and doing something wrong that I had been conducting myself in the most conservative and perfect manner, doing everything by the book and not taking any risk, which ultimately led my ex-partner running rings around me and controlling the outcomes, and my entire life.

I took steps of courage to try to fear less, the potential consequences of not being perfect or meeting his every beck and call. For example, I stopped stressing myself out and dropping everything in my life to scrabble to respond to their legal letters and demands in the unrealistic timeframe they would set for me to respond by. I took my time. I gave it focus when I had availability, and I didn't allow it to consume my entire world anymore. I became very assertive and responded to their correspondence and demands, rather than emotional outbursts, because of a reaction driven by my underlying triggers that were intentionally being probed by them. I set myself a rule that I would not reply to their emails until I had slept on it. This gave me time to process and diffuse the fear that these emails induced and prevented me from reacting with emotion in my reply, which was only giving them more ammunition and power over me. I stopped fearing that if the children were fifteen minutes late answering a Skype call from him because we were out for a special event, that this was okay and not going to cause my children to be taken off me like they once had me believe. I cared less about the consequences while still staying in integrity. I adopted practical control measures to reduce the related stress in the way of establishing a new email account that was solely for legal correspondence and advising them I would only check it once a week.

I took back my personal power. I was in charge. I was no longer a puppet on a string, barely surviving and all consumed with trying to make sure I met his every demand out of fear he would distort everything and try to use it against me in court. I had learnt that the court system is ultimately broken. I had also worked out how to use the flaws of this broken system to my advantage. I was staying in integrity while still supporting and encouraging the children's relationship with their father, but only now it was on my terms.

I ended up finding the courage to write a final letter of offer to his lawyer, advising that I would delete my legal email and that I would not be taking part in any further negotiations. It was basically a take it or leave it offer with a deadline for acceptance before I withdrew from the whole negotiation process permanently, leaving the only option for him to see his children unsupervised and our matter resolved, being he would need to apply to court and go to trial. After three years of intense effort and negotiations, I had extensive evidence to show I had exhausted every avenue for resolve and that many very reasonable offers had been proposed by me with some of these even being accepted by him, only to have him fail to follow through for no logical reason. I had to get myself to a place that I did not fear going to court.

The thought of going to court for our children had terrified me for so long, and this was an avenue for him to keep me as a puppet on his piece of string. Now that I have healed and transformed to a level where I knew I could handle anything and had trust in my truth, I was no longer afraid of court. I had nothing to lose by going to court. We had been down the formal court path for the property settlement and it was all finalised by consent out of trial in the final hour after I had no option but to cave in to their demands. He was trying to do the same now for our parenting matter. He was dragging it out, trying to intimidate and wear me down so I would cave and comply. He did not realise that

I was not the same person I used to be. He also didn't realise that these children ignited more of a fight in me than finances or material things ever could.

There was no way I was giving up on doing what was best for these children and allowing him to use them as pawns for the rest of their childhood. He was going to have to apply to have a court trial if he wanted to push for an outcome for our parenting matter that was different to what we already agreed on multiple times to date. I knew deep down he didn't want to end up back in the full-blown court system, as it required so much money. Money was ultimately his focus, outside of his desire to have power over me. I also knew he didn't actually want to have his children regularly, and that this was largely about trying to get out of his obligations to pay child support and his financial responsibilities to his own children.

Of course, he and his lawyer weaselled their way around my attempted boundary of giving them one last final offer and they responded with numerous manipulative attempts to lure me back into the situation to be pressured and broken down to comply with their demands. However, I didn't allow myself to fall into the crippling fear and disempowerment this time. In fact, I played them at their own game. They had taught me how to play this game. Playing games in this way didn't align with who I was and I didn't particularly like it, but I knew this was survival, and this was about me reclaiming my power and standing up for myself once and for all. This was about me taking a stand for myself for the first time in my entire life. I was annihilated by my family when trying to have a voice or stand up for myself and I was experiencing the same pattern in this process to a more severe degree. This was my time to step into my power once and for all. I had nothing to lose. I had already lost just about everything in my life except my children at this stage. I knew I was a damn good mother and there was nothing of any truth that could ever be said or used against me to discredit my capacity to parent these children well.

In Process Work Psychotherapy, developed by Arnold Mindell in the 1970's, it speaks of a conceptual distinction between the 'primary' or intended and the 'secondary' or unintended aspects of a behaviour or experience of a person. It is based on the understanding that we experience a 'primary process' that are aspects of us with which we identify and relate, and a 'secondary process' that are aspects we find hard to identify or resonate and are trying insistently to enter our conscious awareness.

The primary process of communication and behaviour will be shaped by our conscious norms and values, while secondary processes will include disturbing, challenging or irrational experiences in our life that are further from our conscious awareness and often overtly marginalised[1]. Process Work Psychotherapy aims to integrate secondary or unaware processes into a person's primary, conscious awareness to reduce the disturbance and access its beneficial elements and potential for deeper meaning and personal growth[1]. Since embarking on study in Process Work Psychotherapy, I have been able to explore how I can bring out more of my secondary process into my conscious awareness and integrate these aspects, reducing the disturbance it causes when I experience it in my life. Others can often be a mirror in which we see disturbing traits and energy, that at a subconscious level we may know we are lacking in and that we would benefit from being able to bring out more of in ourselves. I identified the disturbing energy of manipulation, dominance, control and selfishness as aspects that I couldn't access, relate to or adopt in myself. I focused on bringing out in myself, certain elements of these disturbing traits and emerging these into my conscious awareness, integrating this in to my way of being in this situation. I ensured I took only the elements of strengths within these traits, in the way of putting my needs first and not giving consideration to his desires, becoming very assertive and dominant in my communication within the dynamic, and being clever and strategic in how to shut down his intimidation attempts and only focus on what would benefit myself. I didn't integrate the harmful or unethical elements of manipulation, control or selfishness and I stayed in integrity to my values. I was crossing an edge that my subconscious had always kept me away from, driven by underlying limiting beliefs that were not supportive of my evolution and transformation towards a more empowered version of myself. It was what I needed to do to match the energy of this man and stand up to the previously crippling impact that these exact traits and behaviours had had on me for so long. It's important not to confuse this integration process as stooping to their level or lowering your values or standards and becoming like them. It is about stepping into the empowerment and strength that has been laying dormant within your subconscious, unable to be accessed until you have capacity to see the disturbing aspects of others as being a shadow side of yourself to explore, bring to awareness and integrate.

When they tried to intimidate me with legal letters attacking my mental health and threatening they were going to paint me as unstable and an unfit mother to the court based on my reactions they had intentionally baited me into, I would respond calmly and send documented evidence related to his physical assaults on me. I would respond to these attempts at intimidation with one short sentence, stating that the ongoing abuse from him impacted me, so of course I had experienced reactions from the trauma that the experiences had caused. I would then attach photo evidence of the impact of his physical violence, text messages of him admitting he tried to discredit me with false allegations to police to better his own outcome in family court, and other evidence of him admitting physical harm to our children while drunk. I was short and sharp in my response and one hundred percent factual. No emotion and no justification. Pure facts. Needless to say, I have not experienced a further attempt of attack on my mental health or unwarranted criticism targeted at me as a mother in written correspondence from them ever since.

I was feeling more grounded, safe in my body, strong in my beliefs about who I was, feeling I was worthy of having a voice, and stepping further out of the clutches of his control that had me trapped in spirals of fear and disempowerment for years.

My recent transformational shift in my consciousness and awareness also landed with the realisation that I was still playing out my wounding of being intimidated by authority or those of higher status. The wounding of believing I was not equal to or worthy of having a voice or standing up to anyone of authority or higher dominance than myself had played out religiously my entire life. This was a direct passing down of generational conditioning from my mother, who lived this belief her entire life, modelling these fears through her parenting. I experienced the withdrawing of her love or punishment if I ever dared to speak my truth, so I learnt to submit and not speak up to authority. The associating modelling of being submissive, fearing and feeling less than those in authority had become the only way my nervous system knew how to feel. Making the choice to let my lawyers go and self-represent was the best thing I did in trying to regain my personal power in the dynamic. I finally had no choice but to speak my truth, have a voice and put my needs first, without the pressure or fear of being judged, not believed and feeling like a constant burden to my own lawyers. When I stood up for myself, unapologetically and in a controlled and regulated manner, my ex-partner and his lawyer backed down. I felt more in charge of the experience instead of feeling like a complete victim with no voice and no way out.

Initially, I experienced extreme anxiety when responding to my ex-partner through his lawyer and spent the days after panicking about what they would do to squash me back down into silence. As I exercised this assertive muscle and stood firmly in the truth of what I knew I deserved, it became progressively easier. In fact, it became almost therapeutic. It was empowering. My energy shifted and aligned to this sense of knowing I was worthy of having a voice and speaking my truth, and I became more confident to stand up for myself and feared less the authority of potential further court and his lawyers.

I continued to seek regular healing therapies and support for myself, in particular for the regulation of my nervous system. I was still stuck in survival mode and my vagus nerve was almost non-functional after years of extreme stress, but I was seeing significant progress in my healing. The fear-based thinking and anxiety lessened the more space I gave to consciously focus on my breathing, my nervous system regulation and with the consistent support I sought from various therapists. I felt as though I finally had a team on my side who believed in me and one of those team members was myself. I had glimpses of calm, peace, and expansive breathing for the first time in years. I was bouncing back far more quickly from the stressful events that presented in the legal process and was not falling nearly anywhere near as deeply into a trauma response as big or scary things presented.

I have learnt that when our energy is consumed with trying to survive and merely breathe, there is no space for anything even close to thriving or ease and flow in life.

As my nervous system unwound from years of survival mode, as the beliefs that were reprogrammed became my new mindset, and as my heart wall of protection began to slowly dissipate, I not only allowed for deeper connections with others, but I also began to shift and transcend into the new version of me that was deeply connected with myself. This came with the innate knowing of my worth and what I deserve, without needing validation from those people from my past or the new people coming into my future. I could feel I was finally getting closer to finding my way home. It was like I'd been on a life long journey searching for my sense of belonging and acceptance and I was finally connecting in with that feeling of knowing that peace and my soft landing place were just around the corner.

"Speak your truth, even if your voice shakes."
Maggie Kuhn.

CHAPTER 19

Pain into Power, Wounds into Wisdom

Hardships often prepare ordinary people for an extraordinary destiny.

This treacherous journey I have been on has led me to truly find myself and my life's purpose. It has stripped me bare and brought me to my knees to be rebuilt from the ground up into who I was always meant to be. My life is now dedicated to helping those who are still in the trenches and supporting them on their healing journey towards a new way of life.

With this road, there can be heartache and pain. There is also the greatest gift in the opportunity to transform and evolve into a more authentic you, instilled with deep wisdom, immense compassion and such a strong sense of self. There will be a shedding of all that is familiar and comfortable in your world, and this is a vital part of the transformation process. When you live in alignment with your values, stand firm in your beliefs, and hold high standards for your self-worth, you will drift from those people and circumstances that only accepted the version of you that prioritised fitting in with their ideals, limiting beliefs and conditioning.

Healing the trauma we carry is the most profound and life-changing gift we can give to ourselves and our loved ones. We really are the author of our life story. We can stay stuck as a victim in the story of our trauma, or we can choose to create a new narrative in which we can heal and thrive. This is not to dismiss the importance of validation in the healing process, especially for someone who has experienced abuse. Validation is an essential first step towards healing all that has been harmed, fortifying self-identity, and reinstating our voice. Once we have experienced the sense of safety that comes with being seen, heard and believed for our experience, we can then work towards validating ourself and letting go of the need to seek this validation from others. The final stage, and only when we feel ready, is adopting radical personal accountability for our own healing, letting go of the old story, despite what has been done to us.

One of the biggest factors in effectively and permanently healing trauma from the body, nervous system and subconscious mind is our willingness and belief that we can choose to let go of the old story we have created around our experiences. That we have the power to create a new narrative if we so desire. With the right support, we are all capable of reframing our experiences from something that was done to us and that still has a hold over us, to something we experienced that is now in the past and has no control over us, if we let it go.

If we choose to believe we can heal from our experiences, then we can. If we have created a story that we are forever victim to our experiences and we are stuck with the effects, then true and permanent healing will probably not occur. We often gravitate to telling the same story that is anchored in the past. We want to experience the sense of safety and relief that comes with being heard and understood. This is a natural part of processing our experiences, as long as we eventually move forward. A disempowering story can keep us stuck and blocked from evolving through and forward from the trauma. The conclusions that we have made from this place about the world and about ourselves are likely not true. They are more so a reflection of our conditioned lens that held a part in us retaining our story in the way we have. This can cause us to hold on to our trauma and prevent us from true recovery.

So what if there was a way to heal? What if we have the power to change our belief systems, to create new stories, to feel new emotions and take different actions that lead us towards happiness? What if we could choose to be fully committed to being our authentic self? What if we could choose to take action towards healing at the root cause of our trauma and become an empowered creator of our life? Moving towards an empowered state in relation to our trauma and believing we are more powerful than our experiences, is a profound and essential aspect of our journey towards true healing.

When we can clearly connect with the opportunity to strive for post-traumatic growth; a profound personal transformation that follows healing from a highly distressing life circumstance, it can give us hope and place purpose for the experiences that once nearly destroyed us.

Life crises shake up the very foundations of our inner self and identity. The rebuilding of these fractured foundations often has the power to shift the once deeply entrenched beliefs we have and force us to think in a completely new way about ourselves, our relationships and the world. It is like a complete rebirthing. A phoenix rising.

Being willing to confront the effects of a traumatic event once it is over and a sense of safety is established, can lead to a powerful pull towards personal alignment and purpose. It is also important to understand that post-traumatic growth can, in fact, co-exist with post-traumatic stress disorder (PTSD). There can be deep distress occurring from what has been experienced, while simultaneously having radical shifts of beliefs, drivers and the understanding of self and others. It is extremely challenging to evolve amid a crisis when a sense of safety does not exist, but conscious reflection in its aftermath can provide a powerful foundation for growth. We can explore how the experience has changed our mindset and how we appreciate and prioritise things in life differently than before. Maybe our relationships have deepened, or we have had to let go of people who may not be aligned with the version of ourselves we are becoming. We may have adopted a newfound faith or expansion of spirituality.

It is important to note however, that minimising the impact of our trauma to bypass discomfort and prematurely promote post traumatic growth is bypassing the full healing process. This is not likely to result in the deep and authentic transformation that we desire to experience. It is equally important to understand that even in the presence and development of post traumatic growth, it doesn't mean there is an absence of distress or discomfort.

Be patient with yourself as you work through and facilitate the process of your healing. When you feel ready to look outside of what you have been stuck in for so long and derive something positive from your struggles, the possibility for personal growth, life transformation, and alignment to your authentic self and purpose are enormous.

There are some vital elements of true healing from trauma that I have experienced in myself and in my clients I work to support. It is essential to have a trauma centred and holistic approach to your healing. When we take focus away from merely masking the symptoms, and actually address the root cause of the physical, mental, emotional, energetic, and spiritual aspects of a person, we can make enormous progress in the healing of our entire being. Not just the isolated traumatic experience itself, but the deep layers of intergenerational trauma that have likely been filtering down through the generations for many years. When we address our childhood adversity and unhealthy conditioning, we change our entire physiology and allow for optimal health and wellbeing to develop in not only our mental health but our physical health as well. With specific and tailored focus on re-programming our unconscious limiting beliefs, regulating our nervous system, processing our suppressed emotions, discharging traumatic memories and energy from our entire system and clearing the dense energetic imprints we take on throughout our life, we are ultimately healing in the true sense of the word.

CHAPTER 20

THE WAY FORWARD

Through my experience of being in a toxic relationship where narcissistic abuse and domestic violence were prevalent, I know just how charismatic and charming such individuals can be. I have witnessed how these individuals can easily manipulate and lie to receive the special and favourable treatment they expect and feel they deserve, whether from family, friends, legal professionals, psychologists, and anyone else who comes across their path. I also know that dealing with these individuals can leave you feeling ignored, uncared for and unimportant, resulting in significant damage to your self-esteem and sense of worthiness. They will aim to erode you down to nothing, to get you to detach from your soul, from the essence of who you are and become like them. The trauma they inflict can have you turn to fear, lower vibration, and reactions that are not of kindness, respect, or compassion. This is you detaching from yourself and it allows them to infiltrate you further and take control of you. It is only when you are stripped to this lower vibrational state that they can access you energetically and syphon your life force.

Focus on raising yourself up, lifting your vibration, and increasing your energetic frequency. Do the healing work. Don't fight evil with evil. Fight the evil with love. Not love for them, but love for yourself, your network and your passions. When you are deeply connected to yourself and you have a strong energetic frequency, they cannot reach you or control you.

As you embark on your healing journey, surround yourself with people who show you love, compassion and support you, and who are also not afraid to gently hold you accountable and help you grow. For those of you who are in the early stages of a relationship and sensing some potential red flags, check in and reflect on if you are already witnessing repeat patterns of unhealthy behaviours. You may be confused about whether you are perceiving things correctly, but now is the time to really wake up, take action and save yourself from being sucked deeper into the vortex of a toxic relationship. As hard as it may be to let go of the hope that things will improve as the relationship progresses, and as scary as it is to think about being alone and having to start again, it is a vital time to get ruthlessly honest with yourself and tune into what your gut is telling you. Are your boundaries being respected? Are your needs being considered? Is there mutual respect being demonstrated? Do you feel supported and safe in the dynamic? Reflect on the beliefs that may play out for you, how your childhood conditioning may drive the way you feel in this dynamic, and what standard you are accepting and ultimately setting up for the way you will be treated in this relationship.

If you are already well and truly established in a long-term relationship yet feeling trapped and in the midst of trying to survive the trauma from the abuse, it's crucial that you consider commencing some sort of trauma therapy. Trauma therapy can

The Way Forward

support you in becoming mentally and emotionally stronger and to shift you into healthier beliefs about yourself while allowing you to begin to process your distressing experiences and begin to regulate your nervous system. Seek out professional support through relevant legal and government services to guide you through the practical steps you can take to safely exit the relationship and prepare you for the separation process. Knowledge is power. It can be very frightening and disempowering to even think of leaving when you are stuck in the trauma loop caused by the relationship. Start preparing your affairs and putting a safety plan in place before you leave. Don't overshare your plans with friends. Too often when we are in toxic relationships, there are unhealthy friendships that come to light through the post separation period.

If you have already taken the plunge and are in the depth of post-separation abuse, just know there is a way forward and there is light on the other side. It is crucial you seek professional support and healing therapies to help you stay regulated and grounded and to feel like you have someone on your team. A safe space to vent and seek advice is vital during this time. Be prepared to let go of any friends or connections that invalidate your experience, side with your abuser, or cast judgement on you during your time of crisis. Toxic people must go, or they will contribute to you remaining in a traumatised state. Focus on self-care. This doesn't have to be spending lots of money or time away from the home that you may not have a capacity for. It means taking time each day to regulate your nervous system through breathing, meditation or exercise. Self-care is about eating nutritious meals and finding ways to express and process your difficult emotions so not to suppress and make yourself ill. Source some good quality supplements that will replenish the minerals and vitamins that are being diminished due to the chronic stress on your system. Join support groups where you can feel seen, heard, and understood. Avoid jumping into relationships or using substances in an attempt to distract yourself from the pain you are going through. Never give your ex-partner another chance. It is the toughest lesson to learn. Break free of the cycles of being sucked in by manipulation, only to be further controlled and abused.

When dealing with the legal system, ensure you seek representation from a lawyer who understands the dynamic you are in and the type of person you are dealing with. Ensure you request a schedule of costs before they commence representation of you. Don't be afraid to change lawyers if you are not being legally supported in a way that is in the best interest of you and your children. Remember, your lawyer is not your therapist and if you try to download on them, you will end up feeling invalidated and unheard and accruing unnecessary costs. If you are required to present to court, ensure you have done some healing work on your triggers and nervous system dysregulation. The professionals within the court systems are typically not trauma-informed and your reactions and destabilised state can go against you. Remember that anything in writing can be used as evidence in court. Avoid engaging from a place of high emotion or reacting to anything in writing. The less contact you can have with your ex-partner while in the legal process, the better. Work out a safe means of communication for the purpose of discussing your children's direct needs. Consider a co-parenting application as this can assist in the reduction of opportunity for covert abuse disguised as co-parenting attempts. Set boundaries around how much time you spend each week on the legal process. Consider setting up a separate email account and be disciplined about only checking it periodically to give you some reprieve from the stress and anxiety induced from receiving legal correspondence. Continue to work on healing your wounds and moving through your trauma.

The Way Forward

My hope for my readers is that you take away a knowing that there is so much hope for the future. That there is absolutely a way through this experience and that there is light and happiness on the other side waiting for you to embrace it. The post-traumatic growth phase is there for you to explore when you are ready. When you choose to step forward into that next phase, remember that when unhealthy patterns are shifting, especially ones that have been held in your subconscious for a long time, you will face the most fear and resistance. This is because finally being set free actually feels incredibly unsafe and uncomfortable in relation to continuing to play out what is familiar and what you've always known. Change is always hard and change is also absolutely necessary to bring you out of this old life and into the new. Change can be beautiful and exciting if you find the courage to let go of the past.

Whatever stage you are at in your journey of moving away from unhealthy relationships, just know you will get through it. Remember how far you have come and take courage in the fact you are still standing. Make a choice today to take back control of your life and stand firm in your personal power. This life of heartache you have been living does not have to be where your story ends. Crisis is nature's way of forcing change, breaking down old structures and shaking loose negative habits so that something new and better can take its place. Just remember, it is always darkest before the dawn and better times are coming your way if you choose to do the healing work. You are worthy just for existing, you are so loveable just as you are, and you are more than enough. You've got this.

THE DEPTH OF HER SURVIVAL

A wise woman once packed all her stuff and said, "this f@#ked up shit will not be my story", then she left and lived happily ever after. Unknown Author.

Disclaimer:

This is a work of creative nonfiction. The stories, experiences, and events are portrayed to the best of the author's memory. While all the stories in this book are true, the names, roles and identifying details have been changed to protect the privacy of the people involved.

Author Bio

Tracey is a Holistic Trauma Therapist, Mental Health Practitioner, Author and Speaker, with lived experience in navigating the impacts of adversity & trauma. Tracey is an animal lover, an adventure seeker and a devoted mother of 2 children.

Prior to transitioning into the mental health space, Tracey spent almost 2 decades of her career, working in various medical and health & safety roles within the Defence Force and in heavy industry.

Tracey's own life experiences of moving through adversity have led her to aligning with her soul's purpose in supporting others to heal from their trauma. Tracey is passionate about guiding people through resolving the root cause of their mental health symptoms so they can move out of survival mode and into a life in which they can thrive. Tracey supports people through one-on-one sessions, intensive trauma healing programs, retreats, and workshops. Tracey speaks at events about trauma, adversity & wellbeing and lives on the Gold Coast in Australia while supporting people all over the world in her healing work.

REFERENCES

Preface:

[1] The Family Law Act www.austlii.edu.au/au/legis/cth/consol_act/fla1975114/ (accessed 19th March 2023).

Chapter 1:

[1] Buel, S.M. (1999). Fifty Obstacles to Leaving, a.k.a., Why Abuse Victims Stay. *The Colorado Lawyer, 28(10), pp.19.* Retrieved from https://www.researchgate.net/publication/239923010_Fifty_Obstacles_to_Leaving_aka_Why_Abuse_Victims_Stay

[2] Barkley, S. (2022). Psych Central. Retrieved from https://psychcentral.com/blog/repetition-compulsion-why-do-we-repeat-the-past.

[3] Thomas, N. & Westphalen, D. (2022). Narcissistic Abuse: Signs, Effects, & Treatments. Retrieved from https://www.choosingtherapy.com/narcissistic-abuse

Chapter 2:

[1] Stinson, F.S., Dawson, D.A., Goldstein, R.B., Chou, S.P., Huang, B., Smith, S.M., Ruan, W.J., Pulay, A.J., Saha, T.D., Pickering, R.P. & Grant, B.F. (2008). Retrieved from https://www.ncbi.nlm.nih.gov/pmc/articles/PMC2669224/

[2] Jewell, T. & Raypole, C. (2021). What It Actually Means to Be a 'Sociopath'. Retrieved from https://www.healthline.com/health/mental-health/sociopath.

[3] Stark, E. Domestic Violence Victoria and Domestic Violence Resource Centre Victoria, Submission 147, p.34; New South Wales Government, Coercive control – discussion paper, Exhibit 26, p. 8.

Chapter 4:

[1] Gaba, S. (2020). Understanding Fight, Flight, Freeze and the Fawn Response: Another possible response to trauma. *Psychology Today*. Retrieved from https://www.psychologytoday.com/intl/blog/addiction-and-recovery/202008/understanding-fight-flight-freeze-and-the-fawn-response

[2] Sarkis, S.A. (2022). 7 Facts to Know About Narcissistic "Hoovering". Psychology Today. Retrieved from https://www.psychologytoday.com/au/blog/here-there-and-everywhere/202209/7-facts-know-about-narcissistic-hoovering

Chapter 9:

[1] Further information about DARVO (Deny, Attack, Reverse Victim and Offender) is available from Harsey, S & Freyd, J.J. (2020). Deny, Attack, and Reverse Victim and Offender (DARVO)

Chapter 17:

[1] Collins, M. (2001). Who Is Occupied? Consciousness, Self Awareness and the Process of Human Adaptation. *Journal of Occupational Science*, 8(1), 25–32.

Trauma Release Session

Are you struggling with symptoms of anxiety of depression? Do you keep repeating the same life experiences? Are you feeling stuck in a rut and don't know how to shift yourself forward in life? Are you ready to take a leap in moving through your trauma?

Kick-start your healing journey or take your healing to a deeper level with a **Trauma Release Session**.

In this powerful healing session, we will:

- *Identify and reprogram your subconscious limiting beliefs that are keeping you stuck in unhealthy life patterns and sabotaging your progress*
- *Release trapped and suppressed emotions that have become stuck and stagnated within your body*
- *Dissipate emotional and traumatic charge from the priority past distressing events*
- *Regulate and resource your nervous system into its parasympathetic state of rest, digest & heal*

- *Clear energetic contracts and cords that are keeping you stuck in a lower vibrational state, or energetically tied to unhealthy people or situations of the past.*

This comprehensive healing session is designed to create an intensive and powerful shift in all aspects of your being (physical, mental, emotional, energetic, and spiritual).

This is an online session through Zoom or Skype and can be undertaken from anywhere in the world, no matter what your location. For bookings and enquiries, please email traceygracehealing@gmail.com. To learn more about the Trauma Release Session, please visit www.traceygracehealing.com

Phoenix Rising – Trauma Healing Program

Have you experienced adversity and struggle through childhood and/or adulthood? Are you stuck in unhealthy cycles and ways of being and can't seem to break free? Do you find yourself stuck in unhealthy relationships? Do you experience symptoms of anxiety, depression, low self-worth, or other mental health challenges?

This intensive and powerful Trauma Healing Program is designed to create profound changes within yourself and your external life. The **Phoenix Rising – Trauma Healing Program** *can be undertaken over 3 or 6 months and is a tailored & custom program that is designed to your individual needs. Through your program, we will holistically address the root cause of your trauma and related symptoms. You will be guided and facilitated within a supportive and compassionate container to identify, process and release trauma at its cause within the physical, mental, emotional, biochemical, energetic and spiritual aspects of your being. You will be led to align more authentically with the truth of who you are and establish the neuro* *pathways to create a healthy belief system that moves you towards a life where you can thrive. Multiple science based and complementary modalities will be combined to truly resolve the impact of life long trauma, unhealthy conditioning and past distressing experiences. You will leave this program feeling lighter, more confident, empowered, calmer with more inner peace, and motivated for the amazing life you are going to move forward into creating.*

This program can be undertaken online from anywhere in the world, or in-person on the Gold Coast in Australia. Payment plans available. For bookings and inquiries please email traceygracehealing@gmail.com. To learn more about the Phoenix Rising – Trauma Healing Program, please visit www.traceygracehealing.com

Notes

THE DEPTH OF HER SURVIVAL

Notes

THE DEPTH OF HER SURVIVAL

Notes

www.ingramcontent.com/pod-product-compliance
Lightning Source LLC
Chambersburg PA
CBHW030034100526
44590CB00011B/204